THE COMPLETE WORLD OF SPORTS (abridged)

Reed Martin & Austin Tichenor
additional material by Matt Rippy

BROADWAY PLAY PUBLISHING INC
New York
www.broadwayplaypublishing.com
info@broadwayplaypublishing.com

THE COMPLETE WORLD OF SPORTS (abridged)
© Copyright 2013, 2026 Reed Martin & Austin Tichenor

Cover photo compliments of Reduced Shakespeare Company™

First edition: May 2013
Revised edition: February 2026
I S B N: 978-0-88145-557-8

Book design: Marie Donovan
Page make-up: Adobe InDesign
Typeface: Palatino

"If the theatre and drama of the Olympics is not quite enough, take it up a notch or two at THE COMPLETE WORLD OF SPORTS (abridged). A merciless but affectionate satirical take on sporting history."
London Daily Mail—One of the Top 20 Things to Do During the Olympics

"The pacing and timing are crackerjack. It's hard not to grin all night, so give 'em a medal. Who's gonna beat their time in a comic sprint?"
Washington Post

"A fast-moving and deeply funny farrago, a neo-vaudevillian sendup that manages to be both merciless and affectionate."
Boston Globe

"THE COMPLETE WORLD OF SPORTS (abridged) comes through in the clutch. It's extremely smart and funny."
Broadway World

"Daffy! A manically paced collection of one-liners… this frenetic show leaves you with a new appreciation of just how dull life would be had the idea of athletic competition never been invented!"
New York Times

"One sketch rapidly gives way to another, and then another, blending slapstick, sight gags, hernia-inducing puns, and genuine verbal wit."
Boston Globe

IMPORTANT NOTE

The use of the name "REDUCED SHAKESPEARE
COMPANY™" in any way whatsoever to publicize,
promote or advertise any performance of this script IS
EXPRESSLY PROHIBITED.

Likewise, any use of the name "REDUCED
SHAKESPEARE COMPANY™" within the actual
live performance of this script IS ALSO EXPRESSLY
PROHIBITED.

The play must be billed as follows:

THE COMPLETE WORLD OF SPORTS (abridged)
by
Reed Martin & Austin Tichenor
Additional Material by Matt Rippy

For their contributions to the development of the script, the Authors wish to thank:

Dee Ryan; Quincy & Daisy Tichenor; Jane Martin, Campbell & Cian Martin; Don Martin; Alli Bostedt; Matt Rippy; Elaine Randolph; Davey Naylor; Dominic Conti; Jeff Marlow; Mick Orfe; Neil Benson; Opus 3 Artists; Judy Jackson MacIlvaine; Douglas Young; Gillian Albinski; Jennifer King; Scott Phillips, Sonoma County Repertory Theater; Napa Valley College; Charles Towers, Merrimack Repertory Theatre; Spreckels Performing Arts Center, Twitter followers @rabidpsycho, @Computr821, @scurvyjake, and @mamasocrazy; Dodds Delzell, Benjamin Stowe, Chad Yarish; and Yogi Berra.

THE COMPLETE WORLD OF SPORTS (abridged) was first produced by Sonoma County Repertory Theater in Sebastopol, CA from 12 May-13 June 2010. The cast and creative contributors were:

Cast .... Dodds Delzell, Benjamin Stowe, Chad Yarish
Directors ....Reed Martin & Austin Tichenor
Stage manager...................................... April George
Scenic design........................... Scott D Phillips
Costume design.............................Julia Kwitchoff
Sound design...................................Joe Winkler
Lighting design................................ April George
Props ....Elizabeth Bazzano & April George
Wardrobe...................... Rachel Heuy, Laura Tennyson

The show was subsequently produced and performed by the Reduced Shakespeare Company at Merrimack Repertory Theatre in Lowell, MA, from 9 September-3 October 2010. The Reduced Shakespeare Company later toured the show across the U S A and Great Britain, as well as performing extended engagements at the Kennedy Center in Washington, DC, from 5-24 July 2011, the New Victory Theater in New York City from 21 October-November 6, 2011 and the Arts Theatre in London from 17 July-25 August 2012 during the Summer Olympics. The cast and creative contributors were:

Cast ....Reed Martin, Matt Rippy, Austin Tichenor

Directors ....Reed Martin & Austin Tichenor

Stage managers .... Emily McMullen, Elaine Randolph

Scenic design .... Dottie Marshall Englis

Costume design .... Julia Kwitchoff

Sound design .... Zach Moore, Jason Weber, Joe Winkler

Original music .... Jon Weber

Props ...... Elizabeth Bazzano, Alli Bostedt, April George, Matt Rippy

Wardrobe ...... Alli Bostedt , Becca Freifeld, Kelly Purpura

FOR WHAT IT'S WORTH

Although within the published script we use the names Matt, Reed, and Austin, the actors playing these roles in your production should be referred to by their actual first and last names. Sound files for the songs in the script are available through Broadway Play Publishing Inc.

There are a number of topical references in the script. The humor and relevance of these will fade over time so each production may update these few particular spots. This is not to say that scenes should be rewritten, deleted or added (which is, in fact, strictly prohibited) but rather we are giving you permission to change a punch line or reference from "Mike Tyson" to "Steph Curry", or from "David Beckham" to "Simone Biles". Our suggestion for you is, try a reference and if it doesn't work then try something different. Eventually, you'll hit upon something that works. We have found over the years that good satirical targets include politicians with extreme views and/or bizarre physical idiosyncrasies, ridiculous celebrities, pop culture references, and topics that are discussed on the editorial page of your newspaper.

The production elements described in the script are from the original Reduced Shakespeare Company production. Consequently the scenery, props and costumes were all reduced in both quality and number.

We'd encourage you to do the same. The conceit is not only that we are reducing the world of sports, but everything within the production as well. It should look like you are flying by the seat of your pants and not like you've had months to come up with a fabulous design for the show. It's more charming if the whole thing looks like it's being made up on the spot.

In our experience, the script works best when it is performed simply and seriously. That is to say, the script is funny so play it straight. But, most of all, have fun and perform the show with energy and pace. To give you a general idea of the pace: when we perform the show the first act runs about fifty minutes and the second act runs about forty-five minutes. Sometimes, if the audience actually laughs, the show has been known to run an extra seventeen seconds.

Text for the "Sports Tracker" that is used in the show:

(Name of Your Theater or Local Business) Sports Tracker

1. Fastest & Strongest	1. Antarctica
2. Ball & Stick	2. Australia
3. Animal Sports	3. South America
4. Sports in a Circle	4. Africa
5. Warfare Sports	5. Asia
6. Who Can Beat Up Who?	6. Europe
7. Machine Sports	7. North America
8. Occupational Sports	_____
9. Slipping, Sliding & Falling	OLYMPICS

ACT ONE

(Dramatic music plays.)

(The set consists of a cloth backdrop hung upstage. It has two doorways—one stage right and one stage left. The cloth is painted to look like the studio background of a Sportscasting network—bright colors, with a number of television monitors painted on it depicting various sports. There is a "T T S N" logo in the center of the drop between the two doorways.)

(Light up on AUSTIN, *sitting behind a desk. He wears a T T S N ["This Theater's Sports Network"] blazer and tie.)*

AUSTIN: *(Portentously)* It has come down to this.

(Light up on MATT, *sitting behind a desk. He wears a T T S N blazer and tie.)*

MATT: *(Portentously)* Tonight is the night. *(Alternate for matinees: "The time is now.")*

(Light up on REED, *sitting behind a desk. He wears a T T S N blazer and tie.)*

REED: *(Portentously)* There is no tomorrow.

AUSTIN: Never before in the history of athletic competition have so many champions from so many sports competed on the same stage.

MATT: Every sport in the history of the world, from archery to wrestling—

REED: From basketball to bocce ball—

AUSTIN: From championship chess to professional ping-pong, and everything in between!

MATT: I'm Matt Rippy.

REED: I'm Reed Martin.

AUSTIN: I'm Austin Tichenor, and tonight, live from the studios of T T S N—This Theater's Sports Network—in beautiful downtown *(Local city)* you will witness the ultimate spectacle—

(Alternatively, you can use the actual initials of your theater or organization for the title of the Sports network. For example, if you are performing at the Springfield Civic Center the network could be called "S C C S N" —the Springfield Civic Center Sports Network.)

MATT: The granddaddy of them all—

REED: *El chalupa mas grande—*

AUSTIN: The Super World Masters Series Grand Prix Bowl Sudden Death Trifecta Cup Complete Sports Abridgathon!

(Lights up. The guys stand up and come together, revealing sneakers, sports shorts, knee pads, sports socks, etc. They're less bombastic now and—more or less—in their normal stage personas.)

REED: Good evening and welcome to tonight's unprecedented live theatrical sporting event.

MATT: We're going to attempt to reduce every sport ever played in the history of the world. From the Neanderthals who first hit a rock with a stick—

REED: To the Neanderthals who participate in ultimate fighting. *(Alternatively: To Neanderthals like… insert name of an athlete in the news for stupid behavior on or off the field.)* In tonight's one hundred minute broadcast, you're going to see, by our very rough estimate, 3,477.3 sports reduced on this very stage.

AUSTIN: So, let's meet the members of tonight's broadcast team in the *[local hotel]* Up Close And Personal Report. *[local hotel]*, proud supporter of *[local theater]* since earlier this week. *[local hotel]*: When you care enough to say their name three times in exchange for free actor housing.

(REED *poses. The following three introductions describe the actors who originally played these roles. You should adapt these intros to fit the three actors in your production.*)

AUSTIN: In the center ring: from Sonoma, California, the starting quarterback for the University of California at Berkeley's perennial intramural cellar dwellers, the Avant Guards, a former minor league umpire and Master of Fun Arts from Ringling Brothers Clown College—give it up for "Big Daddy" Reed Martin!

(*Applause.* MATT *poses.*)

REED: And in this corner: out of Houston, Texas, weighing in at eighty-seven pounds soaking wet, head thumb-twiddler for the High School for the Performing Arts, former amateur tennis hooligan, haiku-master and part-time crimefighter, the Rubberband Man, the Lanky Yankee—put your hands together for Matt "Slim Goodbody" Rippy!

(*Applause.* AUSTIN *poses.*)

MATT: And from way out in left field: from San Francisco, California, the former East Bay J V Cross-Country Championship Semi-Finalist and Runner-Up; he bats right, he votes left, he swings both ways—try to get excited for Austin "The Poor Man's Will Farrell" Tichenor!

(*Applause*)

REED: Matt, talk to me about tonight's broadcast.

MATT: Well Reed, tonight's broadcast is brought to you by *[notorious local bar, watering hole, or club]*:

Specializing in cheap brew and two-dollar shots. *[notorious local bar, watering hole, or club]*: Keeping local riff-raff hammered since 2007 *(or whatever year the business actually opened).*

(AUSTIN *and* MATT *strike their desks and chairs as they exit.)*

REED: Our Complete Sports Abridgathon is just about to get under way. Our goal tonight is simple: cover every single sport ever played on every continent in the entire history of the world in under two hours. No pressure. Let's go over to Austin Tichenor now to explain the scoring system. Austin?

(AUSTIN *has entered pulling on the sports tracker: a white board attached to a rolling costume rack.* REED *strikes his desk and chair as he exits.)*

AUSTIN: Thanks, Reed. If you'll take a look at our *[local sponsor]* Sports Tracker, you'll see we've spared every expense. *(He uses his microphone to point out the categories and continents on the board [this text is listed on page xvi at the beginning of this script]. The "microphones" are actually just extendable magnetic pointers used by mechanics and available in auto parts stores.)* We've got our work cut out for us. We've got to cover sports in nine categories, from seven continents, and the entire history of sports from the dawn of time until this very minute.

(AUSTIN *stretches a time line ribbon out from the wings. On one end it says "Then...")*

AUSTIN: Or, as we demonstrate with this timeline, from "then"—

(AUSTIN *stretches the ribbon or rope across the stage. It has flags/pennants representing the different eras being discussed tonight. There are eight flags, from right to left: "Now", "20th Century", "1776", "Elizabethan", "Romans", "Greeks", "Cavemen", and "Then".)*

AUSTIN: —to "Now". All of which will lead up to our attempt to cover the world's most challenging and all-encompassing sporting event, and my personal favorite: the Olympic Games. But right now, it's a beautiful night for a ballgame here in *[local city's nickname]*, The pre-game banter is just about over, I have strapped on my game voice, so we're just waiting now for the athletes to burst out of the tunnels—

(MATT *and* REED *burst through black paper which has been taped over the two openings in the backdrop. They wear jerseys from different sports. One stretches, the other bounces, warming up like a boxer.*)

AUSTIN: Ho! *(To the audience)* If anybody would like to clean up the puddle underneath your seats, now would be a very good time. *(Alternatively: "These athletes have been training literally minutes for this!")* We'll begin tonight's Complete Sports Abridgathon with the traditional coin toss. *(He pulls a coin out of his pocket.)* The loser of the previous contest usually calls it; Matt Rippy, you went to a performing arts high school. That makes you the biggest loser. Here's your heads, here's your tails. Call it in the air.

MATT: Heads.

AUSTIN: *(Doesn't even toss the coin)* Tails it is. Reed Martin, you win the toss. You can elect to start the game either historically or geographically.

REED: I wanna start historically, Austin.

(REED *slaps* AUSTIN'S *ass.*)

AUSTIN: Historically it...wow, thank you for that. Now come together... I want a fast match, gentlemen. Lots of good clean abridgement, plenty of jokes below the belt, and may the odds be ever in your favor. Now shake hands.

(MATT *and* REED *stare each other down like boxers before a match, bump fists together, and do a two-handed patty-cake soul handshake as* AUSTIN *says:*)

AUSTIN: Ready, onetwothree—

ALL: Break!

AUSTIN: Athletes, to your marks—

(MATT *and* REED *crouch as if they are about to start a race.*)

AUSTIN: Get set—BANG!

(AUSTIN *uses his hand as a PRETEND starter's pistol.* MATT *and* REED *sprint backstage.*)

AUSTIN: And tonight's Complete Sports Abridgathon is finally under way! Don't miss a second of the action. We'll be calling the play-by-play as the players play so don't look away. Since Reed elected to start the game historically, we take you all the way back now to the beginning of time and a report from our colleague OokOok The Caveman. Ookie?

(REED *enters wearing an animal-skin sash and an unruly wig and beard. He speaks normally, into his microphone.* AUSTIN *exits.*)

(*Note: Throughout the show whenever any of the actors are playing broadcasters or announcers, they wear their T T S N blazers and speak into their microphones.*)

REED/OOKOOK: Thanks, Austin. The Evolution of Sports has been a central part of our daily activity ever since mankind evolved into the magnificent specimen you see before you. After we emerged as bipedal life forms from the primordial ooze—

(AUSTIN *enters holding his smartphone.*)

AUSTIN: Sorry, Reed. Somebody just sent us a DM.

REED: Who?

AUSTIN: *(Comparing the social media profile on the phone with someone in the audience)* Uh, looks like that guy.

REED: *(Reading the tweet)* He's objecting to the fact that I even said the word evolution?

AUSTIN: That's what he said. *(Shrugs and exits)*

REED/OOKOOK: Okay… *(He says the name of the state in which they are performing)*. Mankind and Sports were "intelligently designed" at the same time. These earliest of sports fell into two of the nine known categories. The first was "Fastest and Strongest."

(MATT enters with a club, an animal-skin sash, and unruly wig. He walks on whistling nonchalantly.)

REED/OOKOOK: If a caveman was walking along minding his own business and a bear suddenly attacked—

(AUSTIN enters with a cute toy bear. He growls once and then chases MATT in a circle.)

REED/OOKOOK: Boom! We invented the marathon. In fact, back in the day, you couldn't swing a dead sabre tooth tiger without inventing a new sport. Hurdles.

(Forced to invent a new sport, AUSTIN lies on the floor so MATT has to jump over him.)

REED/OOKOOK: Swimming.

(MATT starts swimming clumsily. AUSTIN exits.)

REED/OOKOOK: Apparently, one really uncoordinated caveman invented the butterfly. And of course, the club came in very handy. Just the mere act of self-protection and daily survival created Category #2: "Stick and Ball" sports such as golf…

(MATT hits a rock with his club, like a golf ball.)

REED/OOKOOK: Ice hockey…

(MATT uses club like a hockey stick.)

REED/OOKOOK: Tennis.

(MATT hits the rock with the club as if he were playing tennis.)

REED/OOKOOK: And when attacked by a predator or tribal enemy, we invented baseball.

(AUSTIN has entered wearing fur covering and fake caveman head. MATT swings the clubs and knocks the fake caveman head across the stage. AUSTIN and MATT exit.)

REED/OOKOOK: Well, let's step over to our *[local sponsor]* Sports Tracker to see how we're doing so far. *(He "crosses off" categories One and Two.)* It looks like we've touched upon category One—Fastest and Strongest— and Two—Ball and Stick sports. And we talked about the invention of sports back 'Then'. But since we started historical, we now go geographic— down to Antarctica and our roving reporter Austin Tichenor. Austin?

(Howling wind. AUSTIN holds a microphone. MATT wears scarf, mittens, and winter hat.)

AUSTIN: Thanks, OokOok. I'm standing here with legendary Antarctic athlete Milo Freezamoff. Thanks for joining us, Milo.

MATT: *(Shivering)* You're w-welcome.

AUSTIN: Milo, You're the champ in the most prominent Antarctic sport. What's that called?

MATT: Surviving.

AUSTIN: Antarctic athletes don't get the respect they deserve in the sports community. Tell the world what you do down here.

MATT: Skiing, snowboarding. This year we added competitive name writing in the snow. It's a men's only sport. There used to be dog sledding, until we had to eat the dogs.

AUSTIN: Rough. How's it going?

MATT: There used to be six of us, but now it's just me and Andy. *(He looks around.)* Andy?! Andy!!

AUSTIN: Congratulations, Milo! You're the last survivor! Any final words?

MATT: Andy was a terrible cook and hopefully a delicious entree. *(Exiting)* Andy?

AUSTIN: Well, there you have it from Antarctica. Over to you, Reed.

REED: *(Entering)* Thanks, Austin. Tonight's Complete Sports Abridgathon is a massive undertaking, but don't worry, we'll guide you through it.

AUSTIN: Our broadcast team has been specially chosen to give you the complete world of sports expertise. I'm the bookish intellectual whose wimpy demeanor masks a deceptively detailed understanding of the complexities of the game.

REED: I'm the ex-jock turned sportscaster with extensive insider knowledge of the game which I'm unable to articulate.

(MATT joins them.)

MATT: And I'm the telegenic eye-candy who'll just stand here and look pretty. *(He smiles broadly.)*

REED: Well, we're off to a quick start so some of you are probably wondering, "Why? Why a Complete Sports Abridgathon?" Well, for me it's about the competition, the courage, the blood sweat and tears. Sports are a drama played out daily by adults and kids, pros and amateurs the world over.

AUSTIN: Reed, for me sports are a study in anthropology. Everyone knows about soccer and basketball, but I'm fascinated by the more esoteric sports—curling, snooker, cheese rolling—and what they can teach us about different cultures.

MATT: And I watched the Super Bowl once. That Janet Jackson had a helluva game.

REED: *(Laughing)* That's good, Matt. But, seriously, what is your favorite sport?

MATT: That would be tennis, Reed. One season I played Little League Baseball until my coach told me I threw like a girl. Which I don't.

REED: Your dad should have given the coach hell.

MATT: My dad was the coach. *(Glaring; as he exits)* Thanks.

REED: You know, Austin, huge sporting events like this always bring out the celebrities and tonight is no exception. If we could bring up the lights here in the arena, perhaps I could wander out here among the crowd and see what famous faces are joining us tonight in beautiful downtown *[name of city]* ... *(He steps out into the audience.)*

AUSTIN: And look how they excited they are that you're doing this, Reed.

(REED asks audience members to stand and be recognized. Grey-haired ladies can be the Golden Girls; a bald older gentleman with a short beard can be Sigmund Freud; a small child can be jockey Willie Shoemaker; he ends by pointing out a distinguished gray-haired man as Martina Navratilova. Just pick people who look vaguely like any particular celebrity and introduce them as such.)

AUSTIN: Wow. It is literally a night of a dozen stars here tonight, isn't it Reed?

REED: Yes, it's like a Laker game but thankfully without the Kardashians.

AUSTIN: Yes, we dodged a bullet there. Okay, insightful insight, Reed, thanks very much. I'm just getting word we have a report coming in now from ancient Greece and the legendary Greek poet, Homer. Homer?

(MATT *appears wearing a toga.*)

MATT/HOMER: Thanks, Austin. Dateline 753 B C. As I reported in *The Iliad*, *The Simpsons*, and *The Odyssey*, the Greeks participated in such ancient sports as the javelin, discus throwing, and nude wrestling... which wasn't actually a sport, but it was a felony. Austin?

AUSTIN: Thanks, Homer. Reed? *(He starts to go.)*

REED: Thanks, Austin. We turn now to baseball, the great American -

(AUSTIN *collapses.* REED *turns.* MATT *re-enters, not sure what's going on.)*

MATT: *(Inaudible)* Dude, you okay?

(This should be played as if this is really happening. They mumble and help AUSTIN *up.)*

AUSTIN: That was weird. I'm fine. Go on.

REED: We should stop.

AUSTIN: No, no. I'll be fine.

REED: Anyway, as I was saying, baseball is America's...

(AUSTIN *collapses again. They rush to his side again and mumble-confer. The audience should really have to lean forward to hear what's being said.)*

MATT: Should we call somebody...?

AUSTIN: No, no...

REED: What does it feel like right before it happens?

AUSTIN: It doesn't feel like anything. It's just suddenly I'm asleep.

MATT: What were you doing right before it happened?

AUSTIN: I wasn't doing anything. I was leaving, and Reed was talking...

REED: I was introducing the baseball sketch.

(AUSTIN collapses again.)

MATT: *(Realizing; to* REED*)* Dude, you can't mention baseball.

(AUSTIN snores.)

REED: *(Waking* AUSTIN *up)* Austin, wake up! You fell asleep while I was talking about...

AUSTIN: Don't!!

REED: Why?

AUSTIN: I hate that game! It's so boring!

REED: *(Shocked)* Baseball isn't boring!

(AUSTIN slumps but fights to stay awake.)

MATT: Reed, you gotta admit, baseball's a little boring.

REED: It's not! It has cool uniforms, rabid fans, fantastic rituals...

AUSTIN: Oh! It's like *Star Trek.*

(REED collapses, unconscious. AUSTIN *and* MATT *help him up.)*

MATT: You okay?

REED: Yeah, sorry.

AUSTIN: Sorry, Reed. Explain to me why base... *(Struggling not to lose consciousness)* ...that game isn't boring.

REED: Because it's not! You've got the pitcher staring down the batter like two gunfighters...

AUSTIN: And eight other guys standing around doing nothing.

REED: Not if he gets a hit.

AUSTIN: Then one maybe two guys get to do something.

REED: On a double-play, three! There's a lot going on in baseball you can't see!

AUSTIN: Yeah, but I like a sport where there's stuff going on I can see!

REED: You don't get it.

AUSTIN: Oh, I get it. What's the most exciting thing that can happen in a baseball game?

REED: A no-hitter.

AUSTIN: Exactly! The most exciting thing that happens is when nothing happens! I'm sorry, but baseball sucks!

REED: You're so wrong. Baseball does not suck. Baseball is... *(He starts to weep.)* Gimme a minute...

AUSTIN: Are you crying?!

REED: No...

AUSTIN: There's no crying in—

REED: I know!

AUSTIN: I'm sorry. I know how you feel. I feel the exact same way about sci-fi/fantasy.

REED: I hate that geeky crap.

AUSTIN: Wait a second. You hate geeky crap?

REED: Yeah.

AUSTIN: Aren't you in a fantasy baseball league?

REED: No!

AUSTIN: Oh.

REED: I'm in three fantasy baseball leagues.

AUSTIN: Dude, you're a super geek.

REED: I am not! *(He begins to hyperventilate.)*

AUSTIN: Yes, you are! I bet you've got bobble-headed action figures, right?

MATT: Yeah, and mint condition rookie cards in plastic sleeves.

REED: So?

AUSTIN: So you're like a Dungeons-and-Dragons-level geek!

REED: *(Getting angry)* Stop it! I am not a geek! *(Out of breath, he takes out his inhaler and sucks in a blast.)* Oh my god.

(REED hitches up his shorts ridiculously high, like a geek, and exits, being chased by AUSTIN.)

AUSTIN: That's right, own it. This is great! We can play fantasy baseball with fantasy characters!

(Lights out except for spot on MATT. Sci Fi/Fantasy theme music begins.)

MATT: Stardate 63827.5. Good evening and welcome to the Fantasy Baseball League Championship, featuring "Derek Jeters Never Prosper" going up against "Resistance Is Futile," an all-star lineup of Daleks, Jedi, Vulcans, Klingons, Cylons, and Futons. Joining me now is the starting pitcher for "Resistance Is Futile", High Commander Spock. Hi, Commander Spock.

(AUSTIN enters wearing the blue science officer uniform, pageboy wig, huge pointy ears, and his baseball glove.)

AUSTIN/SPOCK: *(Flashing the Vulcan V)* I am and always shall be your friend.

MATT: What do you call critics who say a Vulcan lacks the emotion to take it to the next level?

AUSTIN/SPOCK: Illogical. We Vulcans control our emotions so we can open up many wounds which will live long and fester. *(He exits.)*

MATT: With us now is the cleanup hitter for "Resistance Is Futile", from the Klingon House of Mogh, you know him, you loathe him, it's the intergalactic slugger Q'Pow.

(AUSTIN *wears a ridged forehead with long Klingon hair, and carries a bat'leth. He speaks in English, except where indicated.)*

MATT: How do you feel about today's game?

AUSTIN/Q'POW: If we lose to those geeky *petaQ (bastards, assholes),* we will bring shame and dishonor to the Klingon home world. Also, I will lose my sponsorship deal with Johnson's Baby Shampoo. *(He exits.)*

MATT: Okay. Nice guy. Oh, here's a surprise: legendary Jedi warrior Obi-Wan Kenobi has been named manager of "Resistance Is Futile." Just moments ago, "Derek Jeters Never Prosper" won the roll of the twenty-sided die, and have elected to bat first.

(AUSTIN *appears as* OBI-WAN KENOBI.*)*

AUSTIN/OBI-WAN: *(Waving his hand à la Obi-wan Kenobi)* They will take the field first.

MATT: They will take the field first. By Grabthar's hammer, "Resistance Is Futile" are trying to reverse the space-time continuum by sending in Cylon skin jobs to fire up the flux capacitor!

REED: *(Entering)* But here's the 3-2 split-finger from C C Sabathia *(or any other famous baseball pitcher)*— and he strikes out Jar-Jar Binks! "Derek Jeters Never Prosper" wins the pennant!

AUSTIN/OBI-WAN: *(Waving his hand again)* "Resistance Is Futile" wins the pennant.

REED: "Resistance Is Futile" wins the pennant!

(They break apart, excited at how that turned out.)

MATT: Geeks rule!

AUSTIN: Now that kinda baseball, I like.

MATT: Yeah, I was just really worried you were going to mention cricket.

(They all collapse, unconscious. Blackout.)

(REED blows a vuvuzela. Lights up on AUSTIN and REED.)

AUSTIN: Good evening, and welcome to World Cup soccer! Now wait—before all you Americans change the channel, you're going to want to hear this.

(REED blows the vuvuzela again.)

AUSTIN: Not that. Tell them the good news.

REED: That's right, Austin. The World Cup has made some rule changes in an attempt to make soccer more appealing to Americans. First of all, each goal now counts as twenty points. Americans haven't been this excited about soccer since the 1999 Women's World Cup when Brandy Chastain stripped off her shirt and slid to her knees in a sports bra.

AUSTIN/REED: Oh yeah!

(MATT appears with a small soccer ball.)

AUSTIN: The players are taking the field now, Reed. You know, another new rule is that on the opening kick, the goalie is no longer allowed to stop the ball.

REED: And here is the opening kick—

(MATT kicks the ball into the wings and exits.)

REED: AMERICA SCORES!! It's twenty to nothing.

AUSTIN: And it's already time for our first commercial break.

REED: So all you Americans can get to the fridge and the john. We'll be right back.

(Special on MATT)

MATT: Hi, I'm N F L legend Cody Wyoming. Every
year the United Way provides school lunches to over
five hundred thousand needy kids. With your help,
we can continue this valuable program. Last year as
part of my court-mandated five hundred hours of
community service, I spent a week at the Travis Kelce
School of Celebrity Dating. *(Update as necessary.)* United
Way—it works for all of us.

(Lights back to AUSTIN *and* REED.*)*

REED: And—we're back! Austin, explain to me why
America is playing against the U S.

AUSTIN: Soccer's taking its cue from baseball now,
Reed. From now on, like the World Series, the World
Cup will feature only North American teams.

REED: Good thinking, Austin.

*(*MATT *re-enters and sets the ball down on stage. We hear a
whistle blow.)*

AUSTIN: Uh-oh, offsides has been called by referee
Timothee Chalamet in a Speedo.

*(A life-size cardboard cutout of Timothee Chalamet in a
referee-striped Speedo appears in the doorway.)*

AUSTIN: Since America was called for offsides, the U S
will get a free kick—

*(*MATT *kicks the ball into the wings.)*

REED: Escuche belamente boomba boomba boomba!
Gooooaaaall!

AUSTIN: The U S—

*(*REED *blows the vuvuzela again.* AUSTIN *looks, then tries to
speak again but* REED *is still blowing the vuvuzela.)*

AUSTIN: The U— *(He looks again, then speaks quickly.)*
The-U-S-ties-the-game-at-twenty-apiece.

(The ball rolls on and MATT *enters chasing it. He sets it near the doorway.)*

REED: America's going to love soccer now, Austin. Shorter games, commercial breaks, more points on the board—

AUSTIN: Timothée Chalamet in a Speedo, what will they think of next?

(Sounds of gunfire. All three guys duck down to protect themselves.)

REED: Handguns, Austin. Americans love their weapons!

MATT: *(Shooting at the ball, using his hand as a gun)* Bang! *(The ball flies into the wings. Actually, it has been pulled offstage with fishing line.)*

AUSTIN: He shoots, he scores!

(Blackout)

(A particularly martial or gladitorial college fight song plays. Lights up on AUSTIN *wearing Roman garb.)*

AUSTIN: Dateline: 117 A D. The Roman Empire. The greatest empire in the history of empires. It rose. It fell. It struck back. The Romans took the bows and arrows that Cavemen used for hunting and turned them into the sport and skill of archery.

*(*MATT *enters with a toy bow and arrow, and shoots an arrow into the wings. He exits after it.)*

AUSTIN: The Romans used bows and arrows not just for recreation but also for sustenance.

*(*MATT *returns with an arrow through a bag of McDonalds food.)*

AUSTIN: But the Romans weren't the only culture inventing sports thousands of years ago.

(REED *enters bouncing a ball on a hurley stick and wearing a large green leprechaun hat.*)

AUSTIN: The ancient Irish, for example, played a sport that used a stick to hit a small ball between two posts.

(REED *gently hits to ball to* AUSTIN)

AUSTIN: Occasionally the ball would hit a player instead which is why the sport was called—

(AUSTIN *throws the ball and hits* REED *in the stomach. He retches as if he's barfing, and runs off.*)

AUSTIN: Hurling. But nowadays the Roman athletes we remember most are the gladiators. To give you an idea of what it was like, we take you all the way back now to the Roman circus and a report from our colleague Studliest Minimus. Studly?

(MATT *strides on in gladiator garb, including a toy sword and shield.*)

MATT/STUDLIEST MINIMUS: All right gladiators, listen up! I'm gonna teach you how to survive in the Roman Circus. First off, you need a sword and a shield to protect your mid-section—

(REED *bounds on as a gladiator clown: breast plate with a squirting flower attached, clown wig, and red nose.*)

REED/DORKUS MAXIMUS: Hello, boys and girls! I'm Dorkus Maximus and I'm here to show you how to have fun at the Roman Circus!

MATT/STUDLIEST MINIMUS: Stop it! (*To his charges*) Listen, the first thing you need—

REED/DORKUS MAXIMUS: (*Copying*) Listen, the first thing you need—

MATT/STUDLIEST MINIMUS: Knock it off!

REED/DORKUS MAXIMUS: Knock it off!

MATT/STUDLIEST MINIMUS: Stop copying me!

REED/DORKUS MAXIMUS: Stop copying me!

(MATT/STUDLIEST MINIMUS *charges* REED/DORKUS MAXIMUS *with sword and shield.*)

REED/DORKUS MAXIMUS: Stop!

(REED/DORKUS MAXIMUS *does the Curly Howard up-and-down hand motion, confounding* MATT/STUDLIEST MINIMUS. REED/DORKUS MAXIMUS *strikes a victorious pose.*)

REED/DORKUS MAXIMUS: Woo, woo, woo! Are you not entertained? Nyuk, nyuk.

MATT/STUDLIEST MINIMUS: Why you—

(MATT/STUDLIEST MINIMUS *charges* DORKUS MAXIMUS *again.* DORKUS MAXIMUS *stops him with a hand gesture.*)

REED/DORKUS MAXIMUS: Hold it right there, porcupine, stop and smell the roses.

(REED *squirts* MATT *in the face with the flower. A buzzer sounds.* MATT *and* REED *drop character, and confer.*)

AUSTIN: *(Entering)* Ohh, and that buzzer means that's the end of the first quarter of tonight's Complete Sports Abridgathon. Reed Martin, that was a pretty fast first quarter. How do you think it's going so far?

(If something unusual has happened in the performance, they mention it, but usually it's:)

REED: Well, it's a small quiet *(specific day of the week)* night crowd, but these things happen and you gotta play through it. *(He exits.)*

AUSTIN: Yes, you do. Thanks, Reed. Matt Rippy, talk to me about how much you're feeding off this crowd tonight.

MATT: Well, there's a great energy out there tonight. You can't hear it, but you can feel it.

AUSTIN: This is an important game for you tonight. Can you tell us why?

MATT: Well, it's no secret that I know diddly-squat about sports, so I'm just hoping to take it one play at a time, learn what I can, and hopefully work through some deep-rooted daddy issues.

AUSTIN: Okay. Good luck with that.

MATT: *(As he goes)* Thanks, Austin.

AUSTIN: And now, it's time for the Second Inning Stretch!

(REED enters.)

REED: And you know what that means! We need all of you to rise to your feet and join us in singing a very quick version of the traditional *Take Me Out To The Ball Game*. We need everyone to stand up, rise to your feet, and sing along. Just follow the bouncing ball.

(MATT and AUSTIN join REED in getting everyone to stand. MATT holds cards with the lyrics written on them. AUSTIN moves a small ball above the lyrics so the audience knows which words to sing. There's a slow musical intro and then they sing very quickly. The whole song takes about twelve seconds.)

ALL: Take me out to the ball game
Take me out to the crowd
Buy me some peanuts and Cracker Jack
I don't care if I never get back

Cause it's root, root, root for *[local theater]* in beautiful downtown *[local city & state]*
If they don't win it's a shame
'Cause it's one, two, three strikes you're out
At the old ball game
Hey!

(AUSTIN and MATT exit.)

REED: Thank you very much. Have a seat.

(A buzzer sounds, or an end-of-timeout air horn.)

REED: And that buzzer means the second quarter of tonight's Complete Sports Abridgathon is under way! *(He blows his whistle, makes a referee's gesture to start the clock, and exits.)*

("Greensleeves" plays and AUSTIN *appears. He wears an Elizabethan hat and collar.)*

AUSTIN/ELIZABETHAN SPORTS GUY: Friends, Romans, countrymen, lend me your ears for the Elizabethan Sports Report. Dateline 1603— *(Consults yellow parchment)* In the N B L—the National Bearbaiting League—the Bears literally killed the Bulldogs five to nil. There's been a lopsided deal in the equestrian world, with Richard III trading his kingdom for a horse. All's well did not end well for Ophelia, who failed her swimming trials. And it was much ado about nothing for Lady Macbeth at the Westminster Dog Show when her dog Spot was thrown out. Damn Spot! Thank you so much.

*(*AUSTIN *bows. Blackout. Lights up on* REED.*)*

REED: We continue our globe trotting examination of sports from all seven continents by taking a look at the Sports of Australia. Joining me now live via satellite is Bruce McNairy. Hi Bruce!

*(*REED *steps to the side to reveal* MATT *lying on his back on a piano bench with his head sticking through a cardboard cutout of an Australian athlete on a T V screen. It looks like he's upside down, framed in a monitor. His body is covered by a black sheet.)*

MATT/BRUCE: G'Day, Mate!

REED: Bruce! You look like you're upside down.

MATT/BRUCE: So do you, mate.

REED: Fair enough. What can you tell us about native Australian sports?

MATT/BRUCE: Before all our criminal ancestors were shipped here from Britain, Australia was populated by Aborigines who played such traditional sports as rope skipping and boomerang throwing. I'm feeling a little light-headed.

REED: Yeah, you're looking a little flushed. I understand some of these native sports have unusual names. For instance, what can you tell us about goombooboodoo?

MATT/BRUCE: Goombooboodoo was a traditional competition between rival family clans who would grease themselves up and then wrestle. Today goombooboodoo is only played in certain clubs in Las Vegas.

REED: Is it true that in Australia everyone runs around in shorts and sandals?

MATT/BRUCE: Crikey, no. It does get cold down here in the winter.

REED: So what do you wear to keep warm?

MATT/BRUCE: Down undies... *(Faints)* Oohh...

REED: *(Bewildered)* There you have it from Australia. *(He shrugs.)*

(Blackout. A special comes up on AUSTIN.*)*

AUSTIN: And now, the single greatest sports movie of all time.

(Spot on REED*)*

REED: A young boy from New Jersey moves to California where he doesn't fit in and gets beaten up by bullies when he talks to one of their girlfriends. An elderly Japanese gardener jumps into the fray, beats up the bullies, then teaches the boy the power of nonviolence so that he too can beat the crap out of people. The gardener dies and the boy is recruited to play on a sad sack Little League team by an alcoholic coach who hates kids.

(Light out. Spot on MATT*)*

MATT: Meanwhile, down the road a struggling, apparently schizophrenic corn farmer hears voices in his head telling him to build a baseball diamond in the middle of his cornfield. Soon a series of impossible events occur: dead ballplayers arrive, the farmer plays catch with his long-deceased father, Brian sings his song, and four Rastafarians slide in on a toboggan.

(Light out. Spot on AUSTIN.*)*

AUSTIN: Across the country in Philadelphia, a washed up boxer gets a shot at the heavyweight title through a series of far-fetched coincidences. The boxer runs up the steps of the Philadelphia Museum of Art, shouts "Show me the Monet!", and wins an Oscar.

(Light out. Spot on REED*)*

REED: The boxer, the farmer and the kid all train together by running on the beach in slow motion to an inspirational song. Inspired by the drunken coach, the baseball team wins the championship but the kid is stricken with an incurable debilitating disease. He gives a moving speech, saying he's the luckiest guy on the face of the earth, and is promptly euthanized by Clint Eastwood.

(Spot on AUSTIN*)*

AUSTIN: But the crazy farmer signs with the Durham Bulls and falls in love with Susan Sarandon. He wins Best Director for *Dances with Wolves* and lives happily ever after.

(Spot on MATT*)*

MATT: Until *Waterworld.*

ALL: The end.

(They bow formally. Blackout. Latino music plays.)

(Spot on REED *in sombrero and pancho.)*

REED: *Hola. Bienvenidas a continente numero tres—America del Sur, señoritas y señors.* What I said was, "Hello, and welcome to our third continent—America of the South, ladies and seniors." This is where basketball was invented by the Mayans five hundred years ago. Instead of a ball they used a human skull and the winning team was executed. Talk about a sudden death victory. Now how do we define America of the South? It's easy. The Western Hemisphere is divided into North America, which consists entirely of the U S A, and South America, which is everything else.

MATT: *(Entering)* Reed, we talked about this! *(To the audience)* Sorry. *(To* REED*)* Canada is not part of the U S and Mexico is on the North American continent.

REED: Do they speak Spanish in Mexico?

MATT: Yes.

REED: Boom! South America.

MATT: Boom! Latin America.

REED: Boom! They speak Spanish, not Latin. Now, a very popular sport in South America is baseball, especially in Cuba, where it was introduced by American servicemen during the Spanish-American War.

MATT: Another sport introduced in Cuba by the American Military is Water Boarding.

REED: Good point, Matt. *(If the audience reacts negatively, add, "Hey, we're not advocating it. We're just reporting it.")* I'd like to say a few words about bullfighting, a popular but misunderstood sport. Bullfighting falls into Category #3—Sports with Animals—and is a deeply ingrained part of Latin culture.

(During REED's *previous speech* AUSTIN *and* MATT *confer in the doorway.)*

MATT: So you wouldn't say bullfighting is at all inhumane?

REED: Nope. It is absolutely not inhumane.

MATT: Great. Let's demonstrate on you.

REED: *(Not expecting this)* That is a great idea!

*(*AUSTIN *enters, hands* MATT *a pair of horns and a pica, then exits.)*

MATT: Here, put these on.

*(*REED *hands his sombrero to* MATT, *then puts the horns on his head.* MATT *outs on* REED's *sombrero.)*

REED: As you are about to see, bullfighting etiquette is intended to minimize harm to the animal. First are the Picadors, whose job is not to harm the bull in any way, but merely to stick a sharp pica into its neck so that the bull cannot move its head.

MATT: Like this!

*(*MATT *sticks the pica into* REED's *back—the pica has magnets on it, which stick to a metal plate sewn into the back of* REED's *pancho.)*

REED: Ow!

MATT: Reed, that sounds like it hurts.

REED: *(Obviously in great pain, but trying to hide it)* No. Didn't feel a thing.

*(*AUSTIN *enters wearing a sombrero and carrying a large sword, a red cape and a banderilla. He hands* MATT *the cape and the sword, which he conceals behind his back.)*

REED: Next, banderillas are stabbed between the bull's shoulder blades which is an art in itself.

AUSTIN: Yes, it's done gracefully, like this!

(AUSTIN *stabs* REED *balletically. Again* REED *is hurt badly but tries to hide it. The banderilla is also magnetic to make it stick to* REED's *pancho.*)

REED: Ow!

AUSTIN: That seems painful.

REED: (*Still in obvious pain*) No, completely painless. Thank you.

AUSTIN: *De nada.*

(AUSTIN *now takes the cape from* MATT *and comically waves it around* REED.)

REED: Finally, the matador performs several passes with the cape, illustrating that mankind has qualities higher than those of other animals.

MATT: Oh much higher.

AUSTIN: Yes, we're very civilized.

REED: The matador then plunges the killing sword into the bull's heart, causing instant death.

(AUSTIN *waves the cape around* MATT, *then pulls it away to reveal* MATT *holding the large sword.* MATT *runs at* REED *with it.*)

REED: Nooooo!

(*They run offstage.*)

AUSTIN: We'll be back with coverage of South American long distance drug running in just a moment! But first it's time now for the Tiger Woods (*Or whatever sports celebrity is currently embroiled in a sex scandal*) Punchline Update, brought to you by Nike, Gatorade, and McDonalds. Today's punch lines: "Just do it", "Is it in you?", and "I'm loving it!".

(Blackout)

(Dramatic football broadcast type music. Lights up on REED *as Keith Jackson.)*

REED/KEITH JACKSON: Hello everybody, I'm Keith Jackson and welcome to the new season of Monday Night Football as the Dallas Cowboys take on the San Francisco 49ers here at Candlestick Park. Football is a Category #4—Modified Warfare Sport—and a metaphor for the American capitalistic system. Nobody is more likely to be ticked off about that than my new broadcast partners this season. Joining me appropriately enough on my left is the author of The Communist Manifesto, Karl Marx—

*(*MATT *enters with hair and beard as* KARL MARX.*)*

MATT/KARL MARX: *(Heavy German accent) Danke schoen.*

REED/KEITH JACKSON: And to the left of Karl Marx is filmmaker Michael Moore.

*(*AUSTIN *enters in baseball cap/fishing vest/glasses/big padded stomach as* MICHAEL MOORE.*)*

AUSTIN/MICHAEL MOORE: Hey, how are ya?

REED/KEITH JACKSON: Karl, you must be furious that football players sacrifice their physical well-being for the financial benefit of the owners and the media.

MATT/KARL MARX: *Nein. Ich bin ein uber* 49er fan!

REED/KEITH JACKSON: But Michael, doesn't it bother you that football uses so much military terminology?

AUSTIN/MICHAEL MOORE: Like what?

REED/KEITH JACKSON: Bomb, draft, blitz…

AUSTIN/MICHAEL MOORE: Nah. I just like to watch guys fatter than I am run around and fall down.

REED/KEITH JACKSON: But Michael, football exploits the weak and vulnerable, and perpetuates the illusion of male superiority.

AUSTIN/MICHAEL MOORE: Chill out, Keith, I just wanna enjoy the game. Hey Karl, wanna get some nachos?

MATT/KARL MARX: *Der weiner schnitzel?*

AUSTIN/MICHAEL MOORE: Kraut?

MATT/KARL MARX: *Dumkopf!*

AUSTIN/MICHAEL MOORE: *(As they exit)* No, sauerkraut...

MATT/KARL MARX: *Du strudel?*

AUSTIN/MICHAEL MOORE: *Ja!*

(They're gone.)

REED/KEITH JACKSON: We'll be back for the opening kickoff and demonstrations of male superiority after these messages from Depends and Viagra.

(REED exits and AUSTIN enters.)

AUSTIN: *(Putting his finger to his ear to hear)* I'm just getting word we have a T T S N News Flash coming in now so for that we take you over to Scoop Tichenor. Scoop? *(He exits one door and appears in the other, wearing a boater hat. Nasal 20s diction)* Thanks, Austin. This just in: Dateline 1923—Most Valuable Player Babe Ruth has tested positive for beer and hookers. More on that later, but now, we take you over to Scoop Rippy. Scoop?

(AUSTIN exits again, but this time MATT appears in the other doorway.)

MATT: Thanks, Scoop. March Madness update. The N C A A has announced that its men's basketball tournament will remain at only sixty-eight teams this year, not the ninety-six teams as previously thought. This dashes the tournament hopes of both the University of Phoenix Online and the Evelyn Wood School of Speed Reading.

(Football crowd noises. AUSTIN *enters wearing a Tom Landry/Bear Bryant hat and blazer. He carries a rolled-up playbook.)*

AUSTIN: All right, gentlemen, get in here. Gather round.

*(*MATT *and* REED *enter.)*

AUSTIN: Take a knee, fellas.

*(*MATT *and* REED *kneel.)*

AUSTIN: All right gentlemen, listen up. Nobody comes into our house and pushes us around. Unfortunately, out there in the first half, that's exactly what our opponents did. They came into our house and—

*(*REED *raises his hand.)*

AUSTIN: Yeah?

REED: Sir, they didn't come into our house. They came into our stadium. My house is in Iowa.

AUSTIN: *(Holding up the notebook)* Look, I'm just reading what it tells me to say here in the Coach's Cliché Handbook. Now as I was saying, not only did they come into our house and push us around, they rearranged the furniture, went through our drawers and put our wife's underwear on their head.

*(*MATT *raises his hand.)*

AUSTIN: Yeah?

MATT: I don't have a wife, sir.

AUSTIN: I know, son.

REED: And he's not your son.

AUSTIN: Yes, I got that. Thank you. Now you know what this team needs?

REED: Some good players?

AUSTIN: True. But what I was looking for is heart. We just don't have heart.

MATT: I have a heart.

AUSTIN: Yes, I know…

REED: Me, too.

AUSTIN: Yes, I get that…

MATT: Otherwise we'd be dead.

AUSTIN: Well, you did look kinda corpse-like out there. But my point is, you gotta want it, ladies. You gotta want it bad!

MATT: Sir, we're not ladies.

AUSTIN: I know…

REED: And it's "badly".

AUSTIN: What?

REED: Badly. You gotta want it badly.

AUSTIN: What did I say?

REED: "Bad." But the correct English is "Badly". It's an adverb, a part of speech that modifies a verb often formed by simply adding "l-y" to the adjective.

AUSTIN: Thank you, Shakespeare.

MATT: Sir, his name's not Shakespeare.

AUSTIN: No shite, Sherlock!

MATT: And my name's not…

AUSTIN: Stop it! I don't know what went wrong out there. I wanted it bad…

(Either REED clears his throat or the audience calls out "… ly")

AUSTIN: ...ly...and it says here in the Coach's Cliché Handbook that the team that wants it the most wins.

(They all scratch their heads.)

AUSTIN: Which doesn't make any sense at all now that I think about it. The team that scores the most points wins.

MATT: Right.

REED: Yeah, that makes sense.

AUSTIN: You know what? Forget about that. Forget about winning and losing.

MATT: Sir, we forgot about winning a long time ago.

AUSTIN: Great, you're halfway there!

(MATT and REED high five)

AUSTIN: Forget about the standings. Forget about the crowd, what's left of `em. Just go out there and play like you've never played before. So, offensive line, that means you're gonna have to step it up now. Matt can't complete passes lying on his back. Although to be fair, even on a good day, he couldn't hit the ocean from the beach.

MATT: Sir, I could definitely hit the ocean from the beach.

AUSTIN: It's a metaphor.

MATT: I don't think that's a metaphor, sir.

REED: It's more like a figure of speech.

AUSTIN: Stop interrupting! This is not a democracy! All those in favor?

(They all raise their hands.)

AUSTIN: Good, at least that's settled.

(AUSTIN reacts to the audience, only a few of whom usually get the joke.)

AUSTIN: Thank you, three people.

(AUSTIN *shakes his head.* REED *passes his hand over his head, implying that's where the joke went.*)

REED: *(Explaining to* MATT*)* See, what happened was, he said it wasn't a democracy and then we voted. *(Scolding the audience)* You're gonna wake up at three a.m and tell yourselves that's a damn good joke!

AUSTIN: You can tell the good ones. They're the ones we have to explain.

(AUSTIN *looks at the crowd for a beat.* MATT *raises his hand.*)

AUSTIN: Yes?

MATT: Sir, can we get back to the scene, please?

AUSTIN: Yes! All right, gentlemen—

(*A long beat as* AUSTIN *tries to remember where they were.* REED *raises his hand.*)

AUSTIN: What?

REED: Sir, do you have any idea where we are in the show, sir?

AUSTIN: Yes!

REED: Because you were doing a remarkable job of looking like you did not.

AUSTIN: *(Referring to the audience)* They didn't laugh and it threw me.

MATT: Then it's going to be an awfully long night, sir.

AUSTIN: Yes, it is. Listen up, gentlemen, if by some miracle we manage to get through this scene…if by some miracle you manage to cross the goal line in the second half, don't dance around like jackasses, just act like you've scored a touchdown before.

REED: But we haven't scored all season.

AUSTIN: Pretend, okay?! I'm begging you! Just get out there and leave it all on the field. Give me a hundred and ten percent!

MATT: Not possible, sir. The maximum effort anyone can exert is a hundred percent.

AUSTIN: All right, Urkel, fine! Just get out there and play like there's no tomorrow.

MATT: If there were no tomorrow, I'd like to spend my final hours with my family.

AUSTIN: *(Hanging his head)* Okay...

REED: Me, too. *(To MATT)* I love your family.

AUSTIN: Alright, gentlemen. Just get out there and play as best you can. I'd love for you to give me a hun...er, seventy-five percent...

(MATT and REED both look dejected.)

AUSTIN: ...but I'll settle for thirty. And remember there is a tomorrow but life is futile then you die on three, ready onetwothree—

ALL: Life is futile then you die!!

AUSTIN: Let's get our asses kicked!

ALL: Yeah! *(They clap and cheer excitedly as they exit.)*

(Yankee Doodle type music plays. AUSTIN enters wearing a tricorn and holding a scroll.)

AUSTIN: Hear ye, hear ye! This just in. Dateline 1776. Colonists taking Native American sport of Lacrosse as their own. Also taking Native American land as their own. And now, our tour around the Complete World of Sports...

(MATT enters holding a protest sign on a stick. The sign has a circle on it, with a circle around the circle, with a diagonal line through it: "No Circles". Strangely enough, he marches in a circle.)

MATT: Down with circles! Down with circles! No more circles! Circles suck!

AUSTIN: Woah, Matt. What are you doing?

MATT: I'm protesting Category #5—Sports that go in a circle.

AUSTIN: Thanks for straightening that out.

MATT: That's exactly what we have to do to circular sports. *(Chanting)* Hey, hey! Ho, ho! Circular sports have got to go! Join in! Hey, hey! Ho, ho! Circular sports have got to go!

AUSTIN: Why is this such a big deal for you?

MATT: Look, take track and field. Field I love, but track I hate because everyone ends up right back where they started. It's pointless. Lap swimming? Horse and dog racing? Same thing. Tetherball?! I say cut the ball off the rope, have one kid smack it and the other kid chase it. Now that's a sport! Come on, everybody, join in! Only a doofus or a jerk'll play a sport that's in a circle. Everybody—!

(MATT repeats the chant. The audience does or doesn't join in.)

AUSTIN: Stop, stop— They didn't get "democracy", they're not going to get that thing. *(Alternatively: "Wow, they didn't get democracy but they got that thing." Finger to his ear)* But I'm being told we have a T T S N news flash coming in now from Reed Martin. Reed?

(Sounds of African jungle: birds, beasts, drums. REED enters in pith helmet and holding a tablet covered with hieroglyphics. The other two exit.)

REED: Austin, as you can tell from the sounds behind me, I am in Africa… *(Sometimes the audience will laugh at the sound effect here, in which case he says, "Would it kill you to play along?")* … the cradle of civilization, where

I have made an historic discovery. Hieroglyphics on Egyptian monuments indicate that way back in the time of the Pharaohs, they already had neutral referees, player uniforms, and even a way to pay college athletes under the table. But earlier today I made anthropological history! While on a dig in Egypt, I discovered this marvelous ancient tablet depicting an Egyptian sporting champion. *(He flips over the tablet, revealing a photo of Charlton Heston as Moses with the Ten Commandments. He looks at it.)* We think he's Judean. Where are you now, Austin?

(AUSTIN enters as REED exits.)

AUSTIN: Reed, my quest to find the world's most esoteric sport has led me here to Djibouti, a tiny country in East Africa. Young Djiboutians have invented a sport that's sweeping the globe, that combines social interaction with athletic prowess, known as the Djibouti Call. Matt?

(AUSTIN exits as MATT enters.)

MATT: Thanks, Austin. Africa also played host to The Rumble In The Jungle, the legendary fight in Zaire between George Foreman and Muhammad Ali.

REED: Yes, if you want to talk about an ancient and truly international sport, you gotta talk about boxing, the sweet science of two people knocking each other senseless.

(AUSTIN has come back in.)

AUSTIN: Wait a second. No, no, no. Boxing is a savage and barbaric sport. It ought to be banned.

REED: What are you talking about? It's one of the most elemental, mano-a-mano competitions there is.

MATT: He just doesn't like it because he's no good at it.

AUSTIN: No. I'm just saying, what's the big appeal of watching human beings hurt each other?

REED: Are you kidding? Category #6—Who Can Beat Up Who Sports—are among the most popular in the world. Boxing, wrestling, marriage, martial arts… You'd feel different if you knew how to box.

AUSTIN: I know how to box.

REED: You any good?

AUSTIN: That's not the point.

MATT: That means he's no good! Here he is, the great white dope.

(MATT's *head suddenly snaps back as if it's been punched. We hear a punch sound [which* MATT *makes].* AUSTIN *has moved his hand very, very slightly.)*

MATT: Ow!

REED: What happened?

MATT: He just hit me!!

REED: He didn't even move.

MATT: *(To* AUSTIN*)* You hit me, you jerk!

(MATT's *head snaps back again, with the same punch sound. Again* AUSTIN's *hand has barely moved.)*

AUSTIN: I also don't like name-calling.

REED: Austin, you're not allowed to hit people.

(Now REED's *head snaps back. He makes the same punch sound.* AUSTIN's *hand barely moves.)*

REED: Ow!

AUSTIN: You said you liked seeing people hit each other.

REED: Yeah, but you punch so fast I can't see you doing it!

(REED's *heads snaps back again. Same punch sound.* AUSTIN's *hand barely moves.*)

REED: Knock it off!

(MATT's *heads snaps again. Punch sound.* AUSTIN's *hand barely moves.*)

REED: (*Charging*) Why, you—

(REED's *head snaps back again. During the next speech,* AUSTIN *pounds on both guys repeatedly but his hands hardly move.* MATT *and* REED *keep getting punched around, accompanied by the punch sounds.*)

AUSTIN: I don't like boxing. I don't like what boxing turned me into. It's savage—

(*Punch.* MATT *and* REED *react in unison.*)

AUSTIN: Barbaric—

(*Punch. Again* MATT *and* REED *react in unison.*)

AUSTIN: And it's turned me into a monster.

(*Punch. Both go flying offstage.*)

AUSTIN: (*Smiling*) We'll be right back.

(*Blackout. Sounds of cheering fans. Lights up on* AUSTIN *and* MATT *dressed as super sports fanatics.* AUSTIN *wears a W N B A shirt and a helmet that is designed to hold two beers, except that he has diet sodas in it.* MATT *wears a crazy wig and a foam #1 finger, as well as a pink shirt with the Female symbol on it —a circle with a "plus" sign .*)

MATT: Come on, let's go, ladies! Move it!

AUSTIN: Dee-fense, lay-dees, Dee-fense!!

(*Clap, clap*)

AUSTIN/MATT: Dee-fense, lay-dees, Dee-fense!!

(*Clap, clap*)

(REED *enters wearing a mohawk wig and carrying a sign.*)

REED: Comin' through, comin' through. Sorry I'm late, gentlemen. I was putting the finishing touches on this! *(He reveals a W N B A sign.)*

AUSTIN: That looks awesome!

(SFX: buzzer)

MATT: Aww, T V time-out. Okay, tonight's topic: Who's tougher, men or women?

REED: Pfft, men, no question. In the '88 World Series Kirk Gibson limped to the plate and hit the game winning home run!

AUSTIN: Aw, poor baby! Kerri Strug flew through the air, stuck the landing, and won a gold medal with two torn ligaments in her ankle!

MATT: Big deal! Canadian Debbie Brill broke the high jump record five months after giving birth! I forget, how many home runs did Kirk Gibson hit after giving birth? Oh, that's right—NONE!

REED: Alright, alright. What's your favorite women's sport?

AUSTIN: Men's figure skating.

REED: My favorite female athlete, hands down: Shirley "Cha-Cha" Muldowney. Only person—male or female—to win three National Hot Rod Association titles!

MATT: No way! Babe Didrikson Zaharias. The greatest athlete of the Twentieth Century. She dominated every sport she ever played!

AUSTIN: Whoa, whoa, whoa! Patsy Mink.

MATT: Totally!

(AUSTIN and MATT high-five.)

REED: Whoa, whoa, whoa! Who's Patsy Mink?

MATT: Congresswoman Patsy Mink wrote the Title IX legislation which led to schools providing athletic programs for women. If it wasn't for her, we wouldn't be here! Patsy Mink was a woman's athletic supporter!

ALL: Pat-sy Mink!! Pat-sy Mink!!

REED: Wait a second, wait a second. How could we forget? Greatest female athlete? Renee Richards.

(REED *high-fives* AUSTIN.)

AUSTIN: *(Agreeing)* Absolutely.

MATT: Wait. Who's Renee Richards?

REED: Renee Richards was a tennis player who was born a man but had a sex-change operation in 1975.

MATT: That doesn't count!

REED: Are you kidding? Having to sue the U S Open to let you play as a woman? You think that was easy?

AUSTIN: That woman had balls.

(*Buzzer sounds. They go back to yelling at the game.*)

ALL: Dee-fense, ladies, dee-fense! Dee-fense, ladies, dee-fense!

(MATT *removes his pink shirt and hands it to* REED. MATT *has another jersey on underneath. Lights switch to a special on* MATT.)

MATT: Sports update now. Big N F L news from both the Dallas Cowboys and the Baltimore Ravens. The Baltimore Ravens have...the Baltimore Ravens? Wait a second, I'm sorry, time out. Guys? *(To booth)* Could I get some lights? Reed, can you explain to me how come these team names don't make any sense?

(REED *is in the doorway.*)

REED: They make sense to me. Dallas Cowboys. San Francisco 49ers. Baltimore Ravens—

MATT: How does Baltimore Ravens make sense?

REED: Edgar Allen Poe was from Baltimore. He wrote "The Raven." It's a cool reference.

MATT: So they named the team after a depressive drunk?

REED: Yeah. Team names tend to fall into two categories: Brave fighters—Vikings, Warriors, and Pirates—or fierce animals—Lions and Tigers and Bears.

MATT: Oh, my. L A Lakers? Los Angeles isn't exactly known for its lakes.

REED: They were originally the Minneapolis Lakers.

MATT: Or the Utah Jazz? I can't think of any place less jazzy than Utah.

REED: They started in New Orleans.

AUSTIN: That's why I prefer college sports. College sports fans aren't stupid and mindlessly violent like pro sports fans... well, except for... (Name of local college. Getting an idea) In fact...if we want to be more like college fans we should have a fight song.

REED: Why?

AUSTIN: Because we're not violent and stupid.

REED: I'm violent.

MATT: I'm stupid.

AUSTIN: No, think about it. Every college has a fight song that celebrates the greatness, the glory of athletic competition. Our fight song could be something grand, something Shakespearean, like— (Singing a capella)
We band of brothers
We few, we happy few
We fight all others
For honor, glory too

We band of brothers
We answer freedom's call
Stay strong it's all for one
And one for all!

(MATT *really likes this, until he sees that* REED *really doesn't like it.*)

REED: No no no. If we're gonna have a fight song, it should have a Y chromosome.

AUSTIN: What does that mean?

REED: It means it should be short and to the point. *(Singing a capella)*
Fight fight fight fight
Kill kill kill kill
Crush and maim we
Will will will will
Rip their lungs out
Strip their tongues out
Leave them all to die!

AUSTIN: No, no, no…

REED: Break their kneecaps
Smash their fingers
Bring the pain and
Make it linger
Make them cry,
No make them die,
Oh this is my abridged fight song!

AUSTIN: That had a lot of fight—

REED: Thank you.

AUSTIN: But not a lotta song.

REED: It had enough song.

AUSTIN: It was four notes…

REED: That's a song…

MATT: Woah, woah! You guys are over-thinking this.
A good fight song oughta be uplifting and just really
simple, ya know? Something like— *(Singing a capella)*
We gotta go out right now and win the game
Or else our lives will never be the same
But now while our athletes proudly take the stage
We up in the stands proudly refuse to act our age
There's nothing we love more than our sports and
    ball
We rally behind our champions, warts and all
With all of our might we're strong
Sing right along
Everyone sing our abridged fight song!

(AUSTIN and REED applaud.)

AUSTIN: Wow...

REED: That was really good. It sounded a like some
other fight songs I've heard, and that's great.

MATT: Gimme a break, Reed! It's better than fight fight
fight kill kill kill ooga ooga!

REED: Woah, back off, pretty boy! Don't make me crush
you musically.

MATT: Yeah? Bring it, old man! I'll hit you so hard your
hair will grow back! *(You should mock whatever physical
eccentricity the actor playing REED's role has.)*

(AUSTIN breaks it up.)

AUSTIN: Woah, woah, wait a second, wait a second.
Reed—sing that thing you did again.

REED: Fight fight kill kill? I thought you hated that.

AUSTIN: I do. Just humor me.

(REED shrugs and sings his first line twice.)

REED: Fight fight fight fight
Kill kill kill kill

Fight fight fight fight
Kill kill kill kill...

AUSTIN: *(To* MATT*)* Good. Okay now Matt, you sing your thing...now.

*(*MATT *sings his song again, which nicely counterpoints* REED*'s bass line.* REED *begins the counterpoint by re-singing the lines he just sang solo.* AUSTIN *sings his song again, too, and the three guys sing a fantastic a capella contrapuntal trio. When they finish, the audience always applauds as the guys high five.)*

REED: *(Amazed)* That was really, really good.

MATT: Yeah! We're like a quartet!

*(*AUSTIN *hands the guys kazoos.)*

AUSTIN: Let's try this.

*(*AUSTIN *fakes a snare drum intro, then they play a marching band verse on kazoos and do ridiculous marching band choreography.)*

(About halfway through the verse a buzzer sounds. MATT *and* REED *keep playing and doing choreograpy in the background.)*

AUSTIN: Ho! That buzzer means it's the end of the first half of tonight's Complete Sports Abridgathon. We've still got a lot of territory to cover, so we'll have to see what kind of adjustments we make in the second half.

(They sing—this time with new lyrics.)

ALL: Go out to the lobby now and buy a drink
Spend lots of your cash real quick before you think
And while you ladies slowly stand in line
All of you men pee quick and get out in record
     time
Turn on your cell phones, see if someone called
How long you think Reed's been completely

  bald?
Everyone move along

Halftime ain't long
Everyone sing our abridged fight song!
(Spoken) Halftime!

*(Blackout. If your actor is not so follicularly challenged,
you are free to compose your own family-friendly couplet to
replace the "someone called/completely bald" lines. Audio of
the contrapuntal melodies for use in rehearsal is available from
BroadwayPlayPublishing.com. A fully-orchestrated marching
band arrangement of "The Abridged Fight Song" is also
available for license from BroadwayPlayPublishing.com.)*

END OF ACT ONE

ACT TWO

(A bagpipe version of Scotland the Brave *plays. House and stage lights fade, then come up.* AUSTIN *enters wearing loud plaid pants, and a brightly colored golf shirt.)*

AUSTIN: Och, Glenlivet!

*(*REED *enters wearing a kilt, an argyle sweater, and a red beard.)*

REED: Oo aye, Glenfiddich!

AUSTIN/REED: *(Calling for* MATT*)* Och, Jack Daniels!

*(*MATT *enters wearing plaid plus-fours with pink puff balls at the sides of the knees and on the tops of his shoes, pink golf shirt and argyle knee-socks, and a matching plaid tam o'shanter with matching pink puff ball. All three guys carry toy golf clubs with oversized club heads and plastic golf balls.)*

MATT: Sorry I'm late, fellas. I was fussin' over me outfit. I didnae want to look foolish. *(He turns around revealing a pink puff ball on the back of his trousers, like a bunny tail.)*

AUSTIN: No, aye, you look dead great.

REED: All right, laddies, have we got our clubs?

AUSTIN/MATT: *(Holding them up)* Aye!

REED: And have we got our balls?

AUSTIN/MATT: *(Holding them up)* Always!

REED: You know, laddies, I've always wondered, where did they get the name "golf"?

AUSTIN: Legend has it, it stands for "gentlemen only, ladies forbidden".

REED: Ach, no. That's a sexist urban myth.

AUSTIN: It's what I heard...

MATT: But "golf" sounds like the Scottish word "goulf", meaning "to strike or cuff".

AUSTIN: Plus, "golf" is "flog" spelt backwards, and I'm floggin' awful at this game.

MATT/REED: Aye, ye are.

REED: Game? That's a good question. Is golf a game or a sport? I say 'tis a sport.

AUSTIN: Golf must be a sport. It's on E S P N.

REED: That proves nothin'. Most of what's on E S P N is is'nae a sport.

AUSTIN: *(Gasp)* Are ya daft, man? It's E S P bloody N! It's the total sports network! What do you think E S P N stands for anyway?

REED: I don't know.

AUSTIN: It stands for...E...Sports...P...Network! By definition anything that's on there is a sport.

REED: Is poker a sport?

AUSTIN: Aye. It's on E S P N.

REED: That don't make it a sport.

AUSTIN: Aha! But it 'tis a game, wouldn't you agree?

REED: Aye.

AUSTIN: Game, sport. Same difference.

REED: Same difference?! Ye've got haggis for brains!

AUSTIN: I'll not hear a word against haggis!

MATT: *(Breaking it up)* Laddies, laddies, can I help? A game is simply a competition. A sport requires some sort of physical prowess. Some games are sports and some sports are games. But some games are just games and some sports are just sports.

AUSTIN: That was no bloody help at 'tall!

REED: Nay!

MATT: Look, look. Track and field is a sport. Basketball is a game and a sport. Candyland is just a game.

AUSTIN: Obviously, Candyland is a game. If it were a sport, they'd show it on E S P N.

REED: Candyland is not a sport because Candyland requires no physical prowess!

AUSTIN: The World Series of Poker requires concentration, memory and stamina.

MATT: So does watching the *(Local terrible sports team)*.

AUSTIN: Aye, that's true. All right, what about Nascar?

REED: Borderline sport.

AUSTIN: Woah, don't let them hear you say that in North Carolina.

REED: I did'nae say it was'nae a sport. I said I don't know. You know what NASCAR stands for? "Non-Athletic Sport Created Around Rednecks".

MATT: Aha! So it 'tis a sport!

AUSTIN: Aye, it 'tis.

REED: *(Disappointed)* Aye.

MATT: What about hunting?

REED: Not a game.

AUSTIN: And unless the animals are returning fire, it's not a sport!

REED: It's not a sport if things die.

AUSTIN: Ah! Then by your own definition, golf is not a sport!

REED: Why?

AUSTIN: Because people die of boredom watchin' it!

REED: Aye, you're right, Glenfiddich. That settles that. All right, laddies, let's play this last hole very carefully. If you time it just right, you can hit the ball into the clown's mouth.

MATT: And we'll win a free game.

(They put their golf balls on the floor and face the audience.)

AUSTIN: Ohh, they may take our lives but they'll never take our—

(They hold their golf clubs over their heads a la Braveheart.*)*

ALL: Free game!

AUSTIN: Fore!

MATT: Five!

REED: Six!

(They all swing in unison and "hit" their golf balls toward the audience, but the balls and clubs are covered with velcro so the balls stick to the club heads.)

(Blackout. E S P N-type theme music begins again. Lights up on the boys in their T T S N blazers.)

REED: Welcome back to the second half of tonight's Complete Sports Abridgathon. Time now for the *(local business)* Halftime Report. Let's go over to Matt Rippy at the *(different local business)* Sports Tracker to see how we're doing so far. Matt?

MATT: I think it was a great first half, Reed.

(REED indicates to MATT that MATT isn't using his microphone, so MATT takes it out of his pocket and speaks into it.)

MATT: Sorry about that.

REED: It's just that we couldn't hear you there for a minute.

MATT: We had a great first half. In fact, we have the potential to set a Guinness World Record for the fastest Abridgeathon ever. But we're going to have to pick up the pace. Because although we got through six of the nine categories of sports, and four of the known continents, the wild card in the second half is going to be the Olympics.

REED: Austin, that's an almost impossible amount of territory to cover in the second half.

AUSTIN: Not to mention, Reed, the fact that we also have over sixty years of sporting history we still have to deal with. And here's an even bigger hurdle: During halftime, we were warned by the notoriously litigious International Olympic Committee that they own the word "Olympics".

REED: So what are we going to do?

AUSTIN: We're going to call our event the Olympish Games!

REED: Good thinking, Austin.

AUSTIN: Yes, it'll still be great, though—the single biggest sporting event in the world. And it won't just be the Summer Games, not just the Winter Games. It will be the Olympish Games every fan wants to see: Summer, Winter, and Junior all rolled into one!

REED: All right! Second half predictions—Matt?

MATT: I predict we'll see special reports from the towns of Jim Thorpe, Pennsylvania; Green Bay, Wisconsin; and Human Growth Hormone, [local state]. Austin?

AUSTIN: Given our age and physical condition, we were remarkably injury-free in the first half. I'd expect to see a violent death or dismemberment before the night is over. Reed?

REED: I predict we'll see a movie version of the life of former Yankee Manager Joe Torre, who converts to Judaism, marries actress Tori Spelling, and honeymoons in Pearl Harbor. It'll be called, *Tora Tora Torah, Tori Torre.*

(Buzzer sounds. MATT and REED exit.)

AUSTIN: Ho! And that buzzer means the second half of the Complete Sports Abridgathon is now underway. Tonight's second half is brought to you by Southwest Airlines. Reduced fares. Reduced service. All the joys of riding the bus, now with turbulence!

(REED enters.)

AUSTIN: Reed Martin, where in the Complete World of Sports are you now?

REED: Austin, I'm in Asia, the world's largest continent. On the Eastern side of Asia lies the country of Japan, whose national sport... *(He crouches and stomps like a Sumo wrestler.)* ...is played by athletes who are morbidly obese. That's right, Japan's national sport is baseball. Over to you, Matt.

(MATT rides in on a stick horse, carrying a decapitated goat—really just a white bath mat with red paint on it. He wears a turban and makes horse noises, talking to the stick horse as if it's a little unruly.)

MATT: Thanks, Reed. *(To horse)* Woah! I'm on the other side of the continent, on the Western edge of Asia in the country of Afghanistan and I'm playing the national sport of Buzkashi. *(To horse)* Hee-yah! *(He circles around REED.)* To play, you grab one medium-sized decapitated animal—in this case, a goat *(He takes a look at the goat prop.)* ...or a bath mat—and you ride around a series of obstacles—like so—and drop it inside a big empty round thing—like this. (*He drapes it over* REED's *head.*) Sounds simple, right? Well, not with hundreds of other guys on horses trying to do the same thing. (*To horse*) Hi ho, Karzai! Away!

(REED *tosses the bath mat to* MATT *who gallops off.*)

REED: Thanks, Matt. Between Afghanistan in the West and Japan in the East lies the country of China, whose government encourages its one billion citizens to practice Tai Chi and play table tennis. Isn't that right, Austin?

(AUSTIN *enters.*)

AUSTIN: That's right, Reed. Of course, sports in Asia have a long and storied tradition. Over one thousand years ago, the ancient Persians invented both polo and jousting. Jousting, of course, quickly spread to Europe. Let's take a look at this dramatic reenactment.

(MATT *and* REED *gallop on carrying pool noodles and making horse noises. They charge at other using the pool noodles as lances. They hit each other with the noodles, but eventually* REED *repeatedly hits* MATT's *rear end as they "ride" off.*)

MATT: (*As he exits*) Get off, get off!

(*Blackout. Spot up on each guy as he speaks.*)

MATT: "Gold medals aren't really made of gold. They're made of sweat, determination, and a hard-to-find alloy called guts." Dan Gable.

AUSTIN: "You miss one hundred percent of the shots you don't take." Wayne Gretzky.

REED: "You can observe a lot just by watching." Yogi Berra.

(AUSTIN *and* MATT *look at* REED *quizzically.*)

MATT: "The harder I work, the luckier I get." Steve Young.

AUSTIN: "Champions aren't made in a gym.
Champions are made from a desire, a dream, a vision."
Muhammad Ali.

REED: "Baseball is ninety percent mental. The other half
is physical." Yogi Berra.

(AUSTIN *and* MATT *are now a little annoyed with* REED.)

MATT: "It is not the size of a man that matters, but the
size of his heart." Evander Holyfield.

AUSTIN: "It's not so important who starts the game but
who finishes it." John Wooden.

REED: "When you come to a fork in the road, take it."
Yogi Berra.

(AUSTIN *and* MATT'*s annoyance is building.*)

AUSTIN: "Twenty-six times I've been trusted to take
the game winning shot and missed. I've failed over
and over and over again in my life. And that is why I
succeed." Michael Jordan.

REED: "I'd give my right arm to be ambidextrous."
Yogi Berra.

MATT: "Whoever said, 'It's not whether you win or lose
that counts,' probably lost." Martina Navratilova.

AUSTIN: "You should always go to other people's
funerals, otherwise, they won't go to yours." Yogi
Berra.

(AUSTIN *smiles at* REED. *Flustered,* REED *struggles to make
up a quote.*)

REED: "Behind every great man...is a great woman."
Gloria Steinem?

MATT: "Behind her is his wife." Groucho Marx.

(*Blackout.* REED *appears.*)

REED: News and scores update. Professional sports
organizations are following the example of the

Baltimore Ravens and re-branding their teams using
literary inspiration. Some quick scores now: In the
N B A, the New Orleans Metrosexual Vampires
caught the Washington Irvings napping. In soccer, the
Baskerville Hounds killed the Mockingbirds. And in
the N F L, the Chicago Hog-Butchers slaughtered the
Nantucket Pequods. The Pequods were also fined one
hundred thousand dollars for the non-limerick use of
the name Nantucket.

(Lights up on MATT.*)*

MATT: Our globe trotting now takes us to the continent
of Europe, where new research indicates that
prolonged exposure to Beethoven has led Europeans to
play some rather unusual sports. Roving reporter Reed
Martin has traveled to Europe and files this fascinating
report. Reed?

*(*REED *has entered and set two things on the floor in front of
him.* MATT *exits.)*

REED: Thanks, Matt. *(He clears his throat; sings to the tune
of Beethoven's "Ode to Joy.")*
When in Europe you will notice
That they play the strangest games
We will rattle off a few now
Do you recognize the names?
'Course there's football, we call it soccer,
Rugby, cricket, track and field
Cycling, sailing, skiing, hockey
All these sports have wide appeal.

*(*AUSTIN *and* MATT *enter.* MATT *kneels to the right of*
REED, *who is standing.* AUSTIN *kneels on the left.)*

*(They both hold cards on which the names [or partial names]
of these strange sports are written, which they reveal at the
appropriate time in the song.* REED *controls two cards with
his feet, by stepping on a lever that pops the card up from the
floor so that the audience can read it.* REED *controls a card*

*that says "Ball" with his right foot and a card that says "2"
with his left foot.* MATT *reveals the first part of the word
with his card—for example,* MATT's *card says "Korf" and he
holds it next to* REED's *card which says "Ball" to match the
lyrics of the song.* REED *reveals the word "Ball" every time
that word is sung in the lyrics.)*

*(*MATT's *first stack consists of three cards. They are: 1.
"Korf", 2. "Long", and 3. "Bossa" with "Floor" written
upside down on the back of the card that says "Bossa" on the
front.)*

*(*AUSTIN's *first stack also consists of three cards. They are:
1. "Chess Boxing", 2. "Pelota", and 3. "Bull Fighting" with
"Wife Carrying" written upside down on the back of the
"Bull Fighting" card.)*

REED: There's Dutch Korfball and Chess Boxing
Wife-carrying, Floorball too.
Danish Longball, Basque Pelota
Belgian Bossaball for you.
Spanish love to watch bull fighting

*(*AUSTIN *and* MATT *stand and exit.)*

REED: Which does not involve a ball
But the Irish, Brits, and Scotsmen
Have the weirdest sports of all.

*(*AUSTIN *and* MATT *have reentered, each with a new stack of
cards. They now stand on either side of* REED, *again* AUSTIN
on the left and MATT *on the right.)*

*(*MATT's *second stack consists of eight cards. They are: 1.
"Camogie" with "Darts" written on the back of the card, 2.
"Toss", 3. "Bandy", 4. "Quoits" with "Quidditch" written
upside down on the back of this card, 5. "Extreme", 6.
"Ironing", 7. "Bog", and 8. a card with a picture of a leaf on
it.)*

*(*AUSTIN's *second stack also consists of eight cards. They are:
1. "Hurling" with "Sheaf" written on the back, 2. "Caber"*

*with "Toe Wrestling" written upside down on the back, 3.
"Snooker", 4. "Gurning", 5. A picture of a bag of Skittles
on the front, with "Chasing" written upside down on the
back, 6. "Cheese" with "Kicking" written upside down on
the back, 7. "Shin" with "You" written upside down on the
back, and 8. "Snorkeling.")*

*(They manipulate the cards to match the lyrics being sung. It
takes some rehearsal, but is very impressive to watch.)*

ALL: There's camogie and there is hurling
(MATT uses the "Toss" card twice for the next line.)
Toss the caber, and sheaf toss
Snooker, darts and then toe wrestling
They all leave me at a loss.
Bandy, gurning, quoits, and skittles
Plus cheese chasing, Quidditch too.

*(On the word "too" REED reveals the "2" card for the first
time.)*

ALL: Extreme Ironing and Shin Kicking
Bog Snorkeling I leaf to you.

*(The final three cards are a picture of an actual leaf, the
number "2" and the word "You." They bow formally.
Blackout. Rehearsal video of this routine is available at
BroadwayPlayPublishing.com. We hear a short musical
intro then lights up.)*

AUSTIN: Welcome back to the T T S N studio. Let's see
how our attempt to cover the width and breadth of the
complete world of sports is going with my colleague
Reed Martin, who's over on the sidelines. Reed?

*(AUSTIN gestures to the wing but REED sticks his head out
sideways in the upstage doorway.)*

REED: Thanks, Austin. We still have three categories
of sports left to cover. My beautiful assistant Matt
will reveal them now over at the *[local business]* Sport
Tracker.

(MATT *rolls on the sport tracker. Categories #1-#6 have been crossed out, as have the first four continents listed.* MATT *gestures to the board.*)

REED: As you'll note, we've already covered categories one through six in some depth. Category #7, Machine sports, require some sort of mechanical device: bike, boat, car, motorcycle. You gotta love a sport that leaves a big carbon footprint. (*His head slowly disappears out the side of the doorway.*)

AUSTIN: Yes you do, Reed. And I love Category #8— sports based on occupations—which include such obscure and esoteric sports as rodeo, lumberjacking, and the world's fastest brain surgery competition. And finally, there's Category #9, sports that involve slipping, sliding and falling.

(*The buzzer sounds.*)

AUSTIN: Ho! That buzzer means that's the end of the third quarter of tonight's Complete Sports Abridgathon. Matt Rippy, that was a very fast third quarter.

(*To* REED, *who's entering*)

AUSTIN: Reed Martin, break down for us your keys to the fourth.

REED: If we're going to break this Guinness World Record for the fastest abridgathon ever, the keys to the fourth quarter will be to ratchet up the intensity and drive the tempo.

AUSTIN: All right, so we better move swiftly on then to the Olympish Games, the greatest sporting spectacle—

MATT: Wait, wait, wait! Not yet. Why are you so excited to do the Olympics?

AUSTIN: Olympish! We don't want to get sued! The Olympish Games are the culmination of everything we've been talking about tonight: sports from all seven continents, all nine categories, and the entire history of sports all in one package.

REED: And Austin is far too modest to mention this but did you know that the Ancient Greek Olympics were actually invented by Austin's great, great, great, great, great, great, great, great, great, great, great, great times twenty grandfather?

MATT: You're Greek?

AUSTIN: Yes.

MATT: Your last name is Tichenor.

AUSTIN: We shortened it from Tichenoropopopolous. Also, the Olympish Games are the culmination of this middle-aged sportscaster's dream, to pontificate long-windedly about every athlete's rise from poverty and obscurity while killing time between tape-delayed events the internet-savvy audience already knows the scores of. *(He starts to weep.)* Give me a minute…

REED: Absolutely. While Austin takes a moment to compose himself, perhaps I could wrap up our coverage of sports from the continent of North America by saying just a few more words about American gridiron football, the most popular sport in the world!

MATT: Actually, Reed, the most popular sports in the world are soccer, cricket, and rugby.

REED: I'm sorry, Matt. What I meant to say is: American gridiron football, the most popular sport in the world that isn't lame.

(MATT exits in disgust and strikes the sports tracker.)

AUSTIN: *(Recovering)* Reed, rugby isn't lame, it's brutal.

REED: It's a wussy game!

AUSTIN: No it isn't. It's thirty guys running into each other at full speed with no pads.

REED: Yeah, but if you don't have the ball you won't get hit. In real football, every player gets hit every down.

AUSTIN: Seems pretty brutal to me.

REED: It's not. You know what? I'll show you. *(Calling to* MATT, *who's offstage)* Matt, you back there?

MATT: Yeah!

REED: Is there a rugby ball?

MATT: *(O S)* Yeah.

REED: Bring it out.

MATT: *(O S)* Okay.

AUSTIN: What are we doing?

REED: Just watch.

*(*MATT *brings on a rugby ball and hands it to* REED.*)*

REED: Now in a rugby scrum they line up like this.

*(*MATT *and* REED *bend over and put their arms around each other's shoulders.)*

REED: Now Austin, you line up by placing your right shoulder against my left butt cheek.

AUSTIN: Wow, could I?

REED: Just do it!

*(*AUSTIN *does. Now he's blocked by both guys except that we see his head sticking out between them.)*

REED: Y'know, interesting side-note: In a rugby scrum your front line guys don't generally need to be your biggest or your strongest guys because they get a lot of push from the second and third line of men—

AUSTIN: *(From the back)* That's fascinating. Can we get on with this, please?

REED: Right, sorry. So the ball is placed on the ground, and the front lines kick it back to the number eight and blindside and openside flankers. But if the ball gets loose, it's every man for himself—like this!

(REED *places the ball on the ground. All three guys fall to the floor, fighting and wrestling for the ball.* AUSTIN *is furthest upstage and is masked by* REED *and* MATT. *He pulls one arm out of his sleeve so that it is hidden inside his shirt.)*

(MATT *secures the ball and leaps up, celebrating.* REED *and* AUSTIN *stand.)*

(One by one, the guys notice an arm with a bloody stump lying on the floor in the doorway where they had just been wrestling. The guys stare at the arm.)

REED: *(To* AUSTIN*)* Is that yours?

(AUSTIN *counts the arms he sees attached to all three actors and only comes up with five.)*

AUSTIN: *(Embarrassed)* Yes.

REED: You were right. Rugby's brutal.

MATT: Austin, you should have somebody look at that.

AUSTIN: I'll walk it off.

MATT: It's already off!

REED: Austin, you're not doing yourself or your team any favors if you're not one hundred percent.

AUSTIN: No, I'm good.

(REED *crosses to the doorway and picks up the arm.)*

MATT: Dude, your arm is off!

AUSTIN: I'll take an Advil.

MATT: Your arm is off your body!

REED: Sorry son, you played a helluva game. Hit the showers.

(Using the detached arm, REED *pats* AUSTIN *on the butt and* AUSTIN *leaves, taking his arm with him, scratching his back with it just as he disappears.)*

MATT: Does Austin's arm come off a lot?

REED: More than you'd think.

MATT: What are we gonna do?

REED: We need a substitute for Austin. We're gonna have to sign a free agent. Could we get some house lights, please?

*(*REED *goes to a man in the audience and asks him to come onstage.)*

REED: *(To audience)* Could we get a little encouragement, please?

(The audience applauds. Then he says to the volunteer…)

REED: Thanks for helping us out. Where are you from?

(He responds. Even though the volunteer is usually from someplace very close by, REED *says…)*

REED: Well, thank you for coming all this way. Congratulations, rookie. Welcome to the Show.

*(*REED *has brought them onstage.* MATT'*s still in shock and mildly hysterical.)*

MATT: Woah, Reed. What are you doing? We're done!

REED: What are you talking about?

MATT: Austin's arm just came off! We can't do this. I'm sorry, but the Complete Sports Abridgathon is over!

REED: Oh, so you're gonna quit, huh? Just like that?

MATT: No, not just like that. Listen, old man—

REED: No, you listen to me, you young punk! We have not come all this way just to quit now! You think Austin wants us to quit? *(Re: the audience member)* You think this guy wants us to quit?

(REED *encourages the volunteer to say "No" and then high-fives them.*)

MATT: Fine! Then you guys do it! (*He starts to go.*)

REED: Wait a minute! *Wait a minute!* Hang on, son!

(MATT *stops.*)

REED: Do the Olympish frighten you?

MATT: No, the Olympics don't frighten me! It's just that...it's just that the Olympics... (*He starts to weep.*) Give me a minute...

(*After a beat,* MATT *hugs the volunteer.*)

REED: I know how you feel, son.

MATT: The Olympics are huge. With only two of us, they're just so overwhelming. You realize they last sixteen days?

REED: And you realize that if we're going to break this record, we've got sixteen minutes!

MATT: I just can't do it...

(MATT *breaks down, wiping his nose on the volunteer's sleeve.*)

REED: Does this have something to do with your father?

MATT: (*Nodding his head "Yes"*) No! (*Beat*) Maybe.

REED: Matt, listen to me. I'm going to tell you something I think your father never did. You can do this. When you had play practice in drama school, did you ever hear of a guy named Aristotle?

MATT: Yeah. He was married to Jackie Onassis.

REED: (*Encouragingly*) That is close enough. Aristotle's Unities teach us we can't set up an expectation and then not deliver it. (*To audience*) All these people are expecting to see the Olympish, right? (*The audiences cheers and applauds.)* And you know what else? Aristotle thought that sports were one of the highest of human endeavors, that they embody ideals of body and spirit, and that sports can take us out of our shallow selves and make us part of something larger. Part of a team. We're a team, Matt. Do it for me. *(Putting his arm around the audience member)* Do it for us.

MATT: What about Austin?

REED: Austin needs us to do this or he's gonna have to do it single-handedly.

MATT: What about his arm?

REED: Austin will get better. Or he won't. So let's do this for Austin! *(He tosses the rugby ball to* MATT.*)* Whaddaya say. You ready?

MATT: Yeah. I'm ready.

REED: *(To the audience volunteer)* You ready?

(The volunteer responds in the affirmative.)

REED: Let's do this thing!

MATT: What play are you calling first?

*(*REED *does a series of baseball signals, finishing with his hand over his groin.)*

MATT: Right. Urine testing. *(He exits.)*

REED: *(To the audience)* Now unless you've been living in a cave for the last fifteen years, you're well aware of the rampant use of performance enhancing drugs in sports. I don't want to get into this thing and find out we've got cheaters on this team.

*(*MATT *returns with a tray with three sample cups filled with yellow liquid [apple juice]. Each cup has a name on it, written on white tape: "Austin", "Matt", and "Reed".)*

MATT: *(As he enters)* Okay, here we go!

REED: *(To* MATT*)* Okay, Matt, you test yours, I'll test mine—

*(*MATT *and* REED *each take cups.)*

REED: *(To the volunteer)* —and you test Austin's.

*(*REED *hands the third cup to the volunteer who will be hesitant or uncomfortable.)*

REED: I can see by the look on your face the thought of testing Austin's disgusts you. I don't blame you. I'll test Austin's.

*(*REED *takes the cup back from the volunteer.)*

REED: You test mine.

*(*REED *hands his cup to the volunteer.)*

MATT: Urine testing is a very sophisticated process. First, you swirl it—

(They do.)

MATT: Good body.

REED: Excellent legs.

MATT: Then you sniff it—

(They do.)

MATT: Robust bouquet.

REED: With hints of asparagus.

MATT: Then you drink it.

MATT/REED: Cheers!

(They toast, but a buzzer sounds before they drink. AUSTIN *enters and begins to speak. He wears his T T S N blazer and his arm is in a sling.* MATT, REED *and the volunteer set the samples back on the tray.* MATT *sets the tray off to the side of the stage, visible to the audience.* REED *takes the volunteer backstage to prepare for the next scene.* MATT *gathers two more audience volunteers and takes them backstage.* REED *reenters, gets one more volunteer, and takes him backstage.)*

AUSTIN: Gentlemen, stop what you're doing! That buzzer means the fourth quarter is underway! I declare the Games of the *(actual year and actual city in which you're performing the show)* Olympiad now open and I call upon Reed and Matt to gather the youth of the world to assemble now backstage to help us celebrate the *(actual year and actual city)* Games.

(As MATT and REED finish gathering volunteers)

AUSTIN: You know, the Olympish games rarely come to *(Local town/area)* so this might be your last chance to participate...

(As they head backstage with their "volunteers")

AUSTIN: Okay, we have our victim—our volunteers, so for the rest of you, I'd like to thank you so much for all your cards and emails. I'd also like to thank Doctor Don Martin and his wonderful surgical reattachment team, and all the good folks at the *[name of actual local]* hospital: thanks for giving me a hand. And now, let the pageantry begin!

(Parade of nations music begins.)

AUSTIN: First, the parade of nations!

(Four audience members circle through the doorways one at a time. They will each make two trips, holding a small flag of the nation they represent and wearing one or two pieces of clothing that suggests that nation: Uncle Sam hat, sombrero, french beret and white flag of surrender, black derby and umbrella, Mickey Mouse ears and Disneyland flag, rasta wig, pirate hat and Jolly Roger flag [Somalia].)

AUSTIN: *(Announcing)* U S A! Mexico! France! Britain! Disneyland! Transylvania! Jamaica! *(While backstage this volunteer can be coached to strike a Usain Bolt pose in front of the audience.)* Somalia! And now, in a tradition that began millennia ago at the ancient Greek Games, we are proud to present the Abridged Olympish Torch!

(REED *enters holding a small cigarette lighter. He flicks
it and with a gesture encourages the audience to applaud.
*REED *circles* AUSTIN *who holds up a birthday cupcake with
a musical candle.* AUSTIN *had been hiding the cupcake in his
sling.* REED *lights the candle.)*

(The action stops while the music plays once. AUSTIN *and*
REED *mouth the lyrics with hands over their hearts.* AUSTIN
blows the candle out. REED *takes the cupcake and exits.)*

AUSTIN: As always, a moving ceremony. You know,
there are so many new esoteric sports from all over
the globe being added to this year's Olympish Games.
Please stand by while I make sure the satellite feed is
working—

(AUSTIN *glances through the doorway where* MATT *gives
him a thumbs-up.)*

AUSTIN: Okay it is working, we're now ready to take
you, for the first time ever as an Olympish event, to
Pamplona, Spain for the Running of the Bulls!

(Benny Hill type music plays as MATT *runs on wearing a
white shirt and red scarf and screaming followed by the four
volunteers who are dressed the same as* MATT. REED *chases
them angrily in the bull horns threatening to stab them with
a pica and banderilla.)*

(They run in one doorway and out the other.)

(Next, all the audience members and MATT *chase* REED *in
one doorway and out the other. Next, the four volunteers
circle in one doorway and out the other on their own. Once
backstage, they take off their white shirts and red scarves.
Finally,* MATT *runs in one door on his own. He doesn't see*
REED *or the volunteers, so he looks into the other doorway.
Now,* REED *charges in the door with pica and banderilla and
chases* MATT *off stage.)*

AUSTIN: It's never been such a fair fight. Our athletes have done a fantastic job tonight and that's no bull. How 'bout a big hand for our athletes!

(The volunteers have taken off their white shirts and scarves backstage. REED brings them back onstage and has them all bow.)

(AUSTIN exits. The audience applauds as the volunteers take their seats.)

(MATT and REED help folks to their seats then return to the stage.)

REED: One more hand for our volunteers!

(AUSTIN enters and immediately begins the scene. He holds a gavel and a clipboard, and no longer has his arm in a sling.)

AUSTIN: Alright, gentlemen, this meeting of the International Olympish Event Committee will now come to order. All those in favor of making Fencing an Olympish Event signify by raising your right hand.

(AUSTIN and REED raise their hands. MATT does not.)

AUSTIN: What's your problem?

MATT: Fencing is something you put around your yard. I propose we include sword fighting instead.

REED: I propose we include sword fighting, but call it fencing.

AUSTIN: All in favor?

(All three raise their hands.)

AUSTIN: Motion passes. Let me look at my notes here... At our last meeting we unanimously rejected Javelin Catching.

REED: Good.

AUSTIN: Probably a good idea. Badminton is in. Goodminton is out. Boxing is in. Tea Bagging is out.

Let's move on to the Winter Olympish. First of all, somebody stole Larry's sled—

MATT/REED: Aww! What?! No! No! *(Etc)*

AUSTIN: I know, I know. So we're going to have to use Bob's sled. All in favor?

(All three raise their hands.)

AUSTIN: Bob's Sled it is. Now there's another sledding event but our corporate sponsors think the name is disgusting. "Loogee"?

REED: Tell them it's pronounced "Luge".

AUSTIN: Done. Snowboarding—half pipe or full pipe?

MATT: If it's a full pipe they get lethargic and really hungry.

AUSTIN: Half pipe it is. *(The audience usually responds a little slowly to this line, so he says…)* Apparently they're too stoned to get that all at once. Now, for athletes who like both men and women, the Bi-Athlon has been proposed. All those—?

(MATT and REED enthusiastically raise their hands.)

AUSTIN: Okay, that explains a lot.

MATT: We'd like to propose Rhythmic Gymnastics. It goes like this…

(MATT and REED pull out long ribbons on sticks. Music begins. They prance around the stage doing precise choreography with their ribbons. AUSTIN exits, checking his clipboard. After about twenty seconds MATT and REED finish and bow. Blackout)

(A dramatic musical fanfare. Dramatic lights on the guys, one by one.)

REED: The moment has arrived. We have reached the apex, the pinnacle, the final finale of tonight's Complete Sports Abridgathon! These Olympish Games will now conclude with a single thirty-two-sport event. Not the two events of a biathlon.

MATT: Not the seven events of a heptathlon.

AUSTIN: Not the ten events of a decathlon.

REED: No! You're about to witness the thirty-two events of the Olympish Tricotakaidathlon. *(Tricko-tuh-ky-DATH-lon)*

MATT: Never before in the history of mankind has such an event been attempted.

REED: It's risky. It's dangerous. It's life threatening.

(MATT and REED exit.)

AUSTIN: In the event of an emergency, please remain calm and run screaming for the nearest exit. As the clock ticks down the final minutes of the final quarter, let the *(whatever the actual year is)* Olympish Tricotakaidathlon begin!

(Light change. Something like "Nadia's Theme" plays.)

AUSTIN: Welcome to women's gymnastics and the balance beam competition.

(MATT leaps on in wig and tutu, does a delicate balance beam routine but on the floor rather than on a beam—perhaps a cartwheel or a forward roll.)

AUSTIN: *(Now like a golf announcer)* Oh, and a lovely falkow toe-loop there by Mary Lou Komaneci. She was the favorite going into this competition and she has not disappointed. But the Olympish Committee has added an Ultimate Fighting component to this year's event.

(REED leaps on with hat and beard a la Fidel Castro. He starts to throw punches.)

AUSTIN: Here comes the Cuban—Fidel Castrato! What he lacks in grace he makes up for in brute force. Oh!

A textbook haymaker there from the Cuban! Let's see how Mary Lou responds—

(REED *hits* MATT, *who "falls" off the beam and onto the floor.* MATT *kicks* REED *in the groin.* REED *falls to the floor and* MATT *slams* REED*'s head against the floor several times.* REED *is knocked unconscious.*)

AUSTIN: Ooh, Welcome to Ouchtown. Population: That guy. Let's check with the judges…a perfect ten!

(MATT *puts one foot on* REED*'s butt in a victorious pose. Blackout. Lights up on* AUSTIN.)

AUSTIN: Some quick updates from the Junior Olympish, now. There was a huge upset in the Hop Scotch prelims earlier today, followed by a forfeit in the Hide And Seek semi-finals, and the Chinese gymnasts have tested negative for puberty.

(*Light changes to* REED.)

REED: But the big story is freaky phenom Frankie Vesperella, who was eliminated from medal contention in Tetherball earlier today.

(MATT *enters, dressed like a kid.*)

REED: Frankie, tough loss today to the Romanian.

MATT: He's a poopie head.

REED: Now, now Frankie. He beat you fair and square.

MATT: Did not.

REED: Did so.

MATT: Did not.

REED: Did so.

MATT: Did not.

REED: Did not.

MATT: Did so.

REED: Good. That settles that. Back to you, Austin.

(Light back to AUSTIN. REED *and* MATT *exit.)*

AUSTIN: We'll have more of that scintillating interview later. But right now I'm being told we have a new development in the Rock, Paper, Scissor competition. Let's go to the videotape.

*(*MATT *and* REED *run on and play rock, paper, scissors very, very quickly.* MATT *wears a beret.)*

AUSTIN: You can see here the match going pretty much as expected. Of course, the fist pounding on the palms of these youngsters really takes a toll and many of them develop arthritis later on in— Stop! Right there! That is the controversy. Let's rewind that—

*(*MATT *and* REED *move slowly in reverse, making rewinding sounds.)*

AUSTIN: —and take a look at that in slow-motion on the *(Local business)* SloMo Cam—

*(*MATT *and* REED *play the game in slow motion. On the third play,* MATT *puts down Paper.* REED *clearly waits to see what* MATT *puts down before putting down Scissors.)*

AUSTIN: The rules state that each player must finish at the exact same moment, but I believe you'll see the Russian kid hesitate for a fraction of a second to see what the French boy was going to play—and, yes! Right there, the Russian kid definitely hesitated, that's a disqualification, and that's why the French kid is so upset.

*(*MATT *licks his finger and sticks it in* REED's *ear, then they both exit.)*

AUSTIN: Oh, no! That's what's known as a Wet Willay! That has been banned in international competition so now both players are disqualified! This is a huge break for Djibouti who was way behind. *(The audience is usually a little slow in getting this joke, so he says…)* Stick with me if you can.

Heading over to the Aquatic Center now. Here's
Michael Phelps warming up—

*(Phelps's arms appear in each doorway, doing forward
circles. The stage right hand holds an oversized hand-rolled
cigarette. Really* MATT's *arm is in one door and* REED's *arm
is in the other.)*

AUSTIN: He's got an enormous reach, which is why he's
won more medals than any Olympian in history. He
trains hard—

(A puff of smoke coughs through the door as MATT *makes a
huge coughing sound.)*

AUSTIN: And he parties hard. I'm being told right now
that legendary diver Greg Louganis… *(Or any other
diver who's name the audience would recognize)* …is about
to attempt an Olympish first, a high dive into this cup
of water…

*(*MATT *has entered holding a paper cup so it doesn't spill. He
sets it carefully on the floor, then looks up. As* REED *screams
from backstage [the scream of the diver],* MATT *dashes out of
the way as a dummy falls from the ceiling and crashes onto
the cup. Blackout)*

(Lights up on REED, *who enters in a ridiculous toupee and
thick glasses. He speaks with a lisp so that his "S" sounds
like a "Th")*

REED/DUCKIE: *(With a lisp)* Hello. This is Duckie
Wormtonsils reporting from the Big Athalon. Athletes
from the United States of America are known for
having some of the biggest asses in the world. We join
the race already in progress—

*(*MATT *enters and circles the stage wearing shorts that are
heavily padded in the back, giving him a huge protuding rear
end.)*

REED/DUCKIE: And here come Roger Bigtookis!

(MATT *casually scratches his behind just before he runs into the wings.*)

REED/DUCKIE: As you can see, he is a very heavy favorite. It looks like he's wandering off the track and toward the taco cart and into the javelin arena—!

(MATT *enters with a javelin through him.*)

REED/DUCKIE: That's gotta sting!

(REED *leaves.* MATT *removes the two javelin halves and puts them onto his head. He shrugs and exits.* AUSTIN *enters.*)

AUSTIN: We're racing to the finish now, with so many new esoteric sports from all over the world being added to this year's Olympish lineup. These are all actual sports. From Gloucestershire, England—cheese rolling!

(REED *rolls a wheel of orange cheese across the stage towards* AUSTIN *who shrieks and then runs off.*)

REED: From Finland—wife carrying!

(REED *exits.* AUSTIN *runs across the stage, carrying the dummy which is wearing a wig and tutu. As he exits, he bangs the dummy's head against the proscenium.*)

MATT: Oh, that's gotta hurt.

(AUSTIN *enters.*)

AUSTIN: And now from Santa Cruz, California—Ultimate Frisbee!

(AUSTIN *throws a frisbee to* MATT, *who catches it and then throws it into the wings and runs after it.*)

AUSTIN: From Southeast Asia, Sepak Takraw or Kick Volleyball!

(REED *enters, places a volleyball on the ground, kicks it into the wings, then exits.*)

AUSTIN: From Great Britain, Lawn Bowling!

(MATT *rolls a small bowling ball across the stage.*)

AUSTIN: And, from Nintendo Arena, the non-stop action-packed gold medal finals in PacMan!

(*We hear the sounds and music of a pac man game. Lights snap to a special on* MATT *and* REED *with game controllers, staring blankly ahead, mouths breathing and moving nothing but their thumbs. Blackout. Lights up on* AUSTIN.)

AUSTIN: Wow! We'll be back with even more exciting action in Candy Crush and Wordle (*Or whatever silly games are most widely-known when you do the show; alternatively: "…exciting action in Corporate Tax Dodgeball…"*), but right now we take you down to Antarctica for Extreme Ironing!

(*Howling wind.* MATT *wears scarf, mittens, winter hat, and an iron. He mimes ironing clothing, but then gets a bright idea and begins to iron himself to warm up. Next he starts to slide the iron down the front of his body, but before it gets too far below his waist, the light switches to* AUSTIN.)

AUSTIN: Happy ending there for Milo Freezamoff. And now, in the center ring, the only kind of boxing I like, Olympish Cigar Boxing!

(*We hear peppy circus music.* REED *juggles cigar boxes. Big Finish and bow. Alternatively,* AUSTIN *can introduce "Abridged Cycling" and* REED *can do a couple of laps around the stage on a unicycle and then bow. You should customize this event to suit whatever talents your cast has.*)

AUSTIN: We have a very special guest now, the new gold medalist in Quidditch.

(MATT *runs in on a broom. He wears round, Harry Potter-type glasses.*)

AUSTIN: Congratulations, Harry.

MATT: Sorry, old boy, I'd love to stay and chat, but I must prepare for my next event.

AUSTIN: Right.

(AUSTIN *goes as* REED *enters.*)

MATT: It's the only other Olympish event that uses a broom.

(*Again we hear the peppy circus music.* AUSTIN *enters with a curling stone [on wheels]. He pushes it toward the opposite wing and then exits.* MATT *and* REED *sweep in front of the stone until it stops about 3/4 of the way across the stage. Now they sweep even more quickly but the stone doesn't move. Finally* REED *just pushes the stone with his broom and it disappears into the wings.* MATT *and* REED *bow.* REED *exits.*)

MATT: And now, Extreme Curling!

(*Now we hear heavy metal music.* REED *pushes* AUSTIN *across the stage and toward the opposite wing.* AUSTIN *is lying on a skateboard and wearing a wig full of curlers. As he rolls across the stage,* MATT *sweeps in front of* AUSTIN *until he disappears in the wings. The music stops and we hear crashes offstage.*)

(*Terrified by the crash,* MATT *and* REED *run away.* AUSTIN *stumbles back in and awkwardly sticks his landing.*)

AUSTIN: (*Groggily*) We have only two events left in tonight's Complete Sports Abridgathon Olympish Tricotakaidathlon. In just a moment, we'll show you the final sprint to the finish. But first, we are proud to present the United States men's synchronized swim team!

(*"Claire de Lune" plays. Lights up on a large, free standing frame with a picture of waves on it. Slowly* MATT *and* REED *rise from behind the waves in flowery swim caps. They do silly matching arm and head moves as synchronized swimmers, then they sink down and disappear slowly.*)

(*Next we see* REED *rise from behind the water with two orange flashlights—the kind one uses to direct airplanes*

into the gate. He gestures for MATT *to rise from behind the
water. As* MATT *appears we see that he wearing a pilot's
headphones with mic attached. He sticks out his arms as
if they were wings.* REED *gestures with the flashlights for*
MATT *to turn ninety degrees, which* MATT *does. Now* REED
gestures for MATT *to move forward, but* MATT *refuses and
moves as if he's walking down stairs until he disappears
behind the water.)*

*(*REED *shrugs, mimes pushing a button, then sinks straight
down as if on an elevator.)*

(Now MATT *jumps straight up out of the water [sort of like a
dolphin] and then immediately drops back out of sight. Then*
REED *does the same. Finally they both leap up in unison and
then drop out of sight.)*

(Blackout)

*(A slow, dramatic sports theme plays. This entire scene
is done is slow motion. The guys begin as if they were in
starting blocks to begin a race and then run in slow motion
to the edge of the cutout waves. In turn,* REED *and* AUSTIN
dive in and "swim" across the waves. AUSTIN's *swim is a
dog paddle.)*

*(*AUSTIN *gets thirsty and grabs a cup of urine from the tray
which* REED *had picked up after his swim and is trying to
take offstage.* REED *tries to warn him, but* AUSTIN *drinks
without thinking. He chokes, grabs the tray and exits.)*

*(*MATT *is afraid to jump into the water, but* REED *gestures
for him to swim across.* MATT *finally jumps in and struggles
to swim. He sinks then comes up for air and spits water into
the front row, then sinks again.* AUSTIN *enters stretching
the timeline across the stage like a finish line.)*

*(*REED *sees a single hand above the waves and pulls* MATT
from the water. REED *gestures for the two of them to run to
the finish line.* REED *reaches the finish line first but stops
just short, out of breath. He takes a big pull on his inhaler,*

then gets an idea and gestures for MATT *to go ahead.* MATT *can't believe it, but he triumphantly runs—still in slow motion—and breaks the tape!)*

(The buzzer sounds and everything returns to normal speed. Triumphant music plays. The lights bump.)

(The guys strip off their shirts and fall to their knees wearing sports bras.)

REED: Do you believe in miracles?

AUSTIN: My friends, that concludes— *(Pulling out his smartphone)* Wait, hold on. Stop the music. We just got another Tweet sent to our Twitter account, "For the love of god, put your shirts back on."

REED: Good note.

(They do. Update the specific social media platform as necessary.)

AUSTIN: Thank you for coming out tonight. You've been a great audience. We'll be here until *[date]*, so if you enjoyed the show please tell both your friends. Until next time, I'm Austin Tichenor.

MATT: I'm Matt Rippy.

REED: I'm Reed Martin, and from all of us here at This Theater's Sports Network—

ALL: *(They sing and do some simple marching choreography.)*
We covered all sports, we hope you were not bored
To tell you the truth, some sports we just ignored
The show is all done now please get outta here
But not before you stand and give us all a cheer
There's nothing we love more than our sports and
 ball
So rally behind we champions, warts and all
(They slow the tempo and sing in beautiful three-part harmony, then pick up the tempo again for the final word,

"song".)
With all of our might we're strong
Sing right along
This is the end of our abridged fight song!
(Spoken) Good night!

(Blackout)

*(Lights up on the boys wearing gold medals around their
necks and holding small bouquets. They each salute the
audience—*MATT *with a single black glove raised in protest,*
REED *with his hand on his heart, and* AUSTIN *with a Vulcan
V—and bow.)*

END OF PLAY